Pit Trading:

Do You Have the Right Stuff?

by
Dr. Michael K. Hoffman
&
Gerald Baccetti

25th Anniversary
1975-2000

TRADERS PRESS, INC.®
PO BOX 6206
Greenville, SC 29606

Books and Gifts
for Investors and Traders

TRADERS PRESS, INC.®
PO BOX 6206
Greenville, SC 29606

Publishers of:

A Complete Guide to Trading Profits (Paris)
A Professional Look at S&P Day Trading (Trivette)
Ask Mr. EasyLanguage (Tennis)
Beginner's Guide to Computer Assisted Trading (Alexander)
Channels and Cycles: A Tribute to J.M. Hurst (Millard)
Chart Reading for Professional Traders (Jenkins)
Commodity Spreads: Analysis, Selection and Trading Techniques (Smith)
Comparison of Twelve Technical Trading Systems (Lukac, Brorsen, & Irwin)
Day Trading with Short Term Price Patterns (Crabel)
Fibonacci Ratios with Pattern Recognition (Pesavento)
Geometry of Stock Market Profits (Jenkins)
Harmonic Vibrations (Pesavento)
How to Trade in Stocks (Livermore)
Hurst Cycles Course (J.M. Hurst)
Jesse Livermore: Speculator King (Sarnoff)
Magic of Moving Averages (Lowry)
Planetary Harmonics of Speculative Markets (Pesavento)
Point & Figure Charting (Aby)
Point & Figure Charting: Commodity and Stock Trading Techniques (Zieg)
Profitable Grain Trading (Ainsworth)
Profitable Pattern for Stock Trading (Pesavento)
Reminiscences of a Stock Operator (Lefevre)
Stock Market Trading Systems (Appel & Hitschler)
Stock Patterns for Day Trading (Rudd)
Study Helps in Point & Figure Techniques (Wheelan)
Technically Speaking (Wilkinson)
Technical Trading Systems for Commodities and Stocks (Patel)
The Professional Commodity Trader (Kroll)
The Taylor Trading Technique (Taylor)
The Traders (Kleinfeld)
The Trading Rule That Can Make You Rich* (Dobson)
Traders Guide to Technical Analysis (Hardy)
Trading Secrets of the Inner Circle (Goodwin)
Trading S&P Futures and Options (Lloyd)
Understanding Bollinger Bands (Dobson)
Understanding Fibonacci Numbers (Dobson)
Viewpoints of a Commodity Trader (Longstreet)
Wall Street Ventures & Adventures Through Forty Years (Wyckoff)
Winning Market Systems (Appel)

Please contact **Traders Press** to receive our current 100 page catalog
describing these and many other books and gifts of interest to
investors and traders.

800-927-8222 ~ Fax 864-298-0221 ~ 864-298-0222 tradersprs@aol.com
http://www.traderspress.com

Copyright© 1999 by Michael K. Hoffman & Gerald Baccetti

ISBN: 0-934380-52-X
Published July, 1999

25th Anniversary
1975-2000

TRADERS PRESS, INC.®
PO Box 6206
GREENVILLE, SC 29606

~Acknowledgments ~

We would like to thank our wives *Shari Hoffman* and *Gail Baccetti* for their assistance, encouragement and love. With their support this challenge, like all other challenges that we have faced, has been worthwhile and meaningful.

Since the entire project was completed at Gerry's home, Gerry's wife, Gail deserves special mention for her extra duties on the weekend that included feedback, refereeing and always providing an unbiased opinion.

I would like to thank *Ed Brenner* who helped me with the original outline of the book many, many years ago; *Mary Holmes* who encouraged us to continue and complete the work; *John Goodwin* for his artwork on the cover; *Bill Falloon* whose words of advice made a great deal of sense to two inexperienced authors; *Stephani Radkay* and *Danielle Hoffman* for time spent critiquing the work prior to going to press.

We would be remiss if we did not thank each other for putting up with each other's quirks, strengths and weaknesses. Coauthoring a book is no simple task. Gerry's knowledge of futures and options as well as his ability to instantaneously put thoughts into words have enabled a long time undertaking to become a reality.

Finally, we would like to thank all those at **Traders Press**: *Ed Dobson, Margaret Ros Hudson,* **and** *Teresa Darty Alligood* for their enthusiastic endorsement, patience and overall effort to bring this book to fruition. We do not believe that *Margaret* and *Teresa* have ever had an experience like the one they had with us. It is our hope that they recover from the undertaking.

Mickey Hoffman and Gerry Baccetti

~Dedication~

This book is dedicated to past, present
and future traders who have competed
and continue to compete in the trading pits
of the exchanges all over the world.

~Foreword~

Before you begin reading *Pit Trading: Do You Have the Right Stuff?* we would like to briefly share with you the history of how Gerry and I began our careers in trading and why we have written this book.

I started my career in trading at the age of thirty-seven. Prior to becoming a trader, I was a teacher, head coach, and vice principal of a high school in a suburb of Chicago. Gerry began his career at the age of thirty. Gerry was an English teacher at an elementary school in a suburb of Chicago. Like myself, Gerry was dedicated to the profession of teaching, but....

For many years I had expended a great deal of energy to prepare myself for a career that I believed would satisfy my inner needs. I loved being in Education, where I could actually see the benefits of my contribution to young people, but I began to realize that the time spent in helping other people's children and the dollars earned for my own family were not commensurate. What worried me was the pervasive question: how was I going to afford my children's education? My wife and I would have to borrow heavily to send our children to college.

In 1981, fate played her hand in my life by reuniting me with two boyhood friends. Both were traders at the **Chicago Mercantile Exchange**. After many conversations concerning their respective successes, a six month stint as a yellow coated nonworking clerk on the Exchange floor, and the willingness of these two friends to assist in launching my trading career, I made my decision to become a commodity futures trader. Enticed by the dollars and the freedom, I was hooked. Without training, and completely unprepared, I began trading. This was not a great move, since I was giving up an assured income, a relatively stable future, and a life of tranquility. I started my new career along with one hundred other novice traders. Ten years later, I believe I was the only one of the original one hundred who remained in the business.

Gerry had not really considered changing careers until he met an old friend who was trading options at the **Chicago Board of Options Exchange (CBOE)**. Seduced by the possibility of earning a better living for himself, he spent an entire summer watching his friend trade and learning the business on the floor of the **CBOE**. Agonizing over the question of whether or not to leave the career he believed he was born to pursue, this eternal optimist cashed in his teacher retirement fund to subsidize his trading career. His decision would lead to a whirlwind ride that would last no less than two decades.

When I began my trading career, I discovered, after making the commitment to become a trader, that there was no formal organized educational track. Unfortunately for me, my friends at the Exchange were too busy, too immersed in their own lives to help me learn what trading was all about. Similar to my Doctoral dissertation work, I was again to depend solely on my own initiative to succeed or fail. After realizing the difficulty of the undertaking. I made two commitments: first, to do what was humanly possible to learn to trade by trading, reading, thinking, and asking questions; second, to eventually develop an educational program for all those who would be interested in learning about a career in trading.

In 1990, I began developing my educational program by teaching two courses at the **Chicago Mercantile Exchange**, *Be A Professional Pit Trader* and *Speed Scalping*. In 1991, I developed a Saturday seminar entitled *Pit Trading 101* for all those interested in pursuing a career in trading. Today, I continue to conduct Saturday seminars every other month. Also, in 1991, I developed a school for training traders called the **University of Trading**. Today, the program has grown to include three levels of learning to trade, BASIC, INTERMEDIATE, AND ADVANCED, taught by twenty-eight instructors. The concept of educating new traders has inspired the development of a software program entitled *The Trader Improvement Series*, to assist traders in reviewing their trading performance after each trading day, and the trading book you are about to read: *Pit Trading: Do You Have the Right Stuff?*

Gerry and I hope that our book will give you additional insight into what we believe has been a somewhat mysterious and difficult to understand endeavor. As of late, there have been many books written about trading. Unlike many of these, we believe ours will afford you an opportunity to learn and comprehend the actions of a pit trader as he executes his system of trading.

At this time, Gerry and I want to wish you good luck and good fortune. We thank you for reading our book and look forward to the possibility of meeting you in one of our courses or hearing from you.

Dr. Michael K. Hoffman, "*Mickey*" is President of **UOT Financial Services,** a commodity and options trading firm in Chicago that caters to new and experienced traders. A member of the **Chicago Mercantile Exchange (1981)** and the **Chicago Board of Trade** (1996), *Mickey* is a former agricultural, currency, and interest rate trader (1981-1987) and Broker in the **Standard & Poor 500** (1987-1992). At the **Chicago Mercantile Exchange**, his courses and weekend seminars, *Be a Professional Pit Trader, Speed Scalping* and *Pit Trading 101,* have introduced hundreds of potential traders to the world of futures and options trading. He has also developed the **University of Trading**, a school that specializes in the training of futures and options traders.

Dr. Hoffman earned a Bachelor's of Science Degree from the **University of Illinois** in Champaign (1965). He received a Masters of Arts Degree in Educational Administration from **Roosevelt University** in Chicago (1969). He was awarded a doctorate in Administration, Higher and Continuing Education at **University of Illinois** in Champaign (1978).

Dr. Hoffman lives in Northbrook, Illinois with his wife *Shari. Stephanie*, his oldest daughter, is a floor broker in the **NASDAQ 100** at the **Chicago Mercantile Exchange,** and his son-in-law, *Michael Radkay,* is a U.S. Treasury Bond Trader at the **Chicago Board of Trade**. His youngest daughter, *Danielle*, is a Trader Assistant at the **Chicago Board of Options Exchange**.

~*Biography*~
Gerry

Gerry Baccetti has been an options trader for the past 21 years. For the better part of a decade, he was enjoying a successful career as an educator, when he was persuaded to accompany a friend to the floor of the **Chicago Board Options Exchange** during a summer vacation. "From that point on, I was hooked!" He remembers fondly. Leaving the security of a tenured teaching position, *Gerry* cashed in his teacher's retirement fund to bankroll his trading account. *"In retrospect, it seems like a crazy thing to do, but I would do it all over again, if given the same opportunity," he stated with a wry smile on his face. "Trading has been a whirlwind ride of ups and downs, but it has afforded me a chance to learn and understand that which makes me who I am."*

Gerry has been a trading member on the **Midwest** (now **Chicago**) **Stock Exchange Options Floor**, the **Chicago Board Options Exchange**, and **The Chicago Board of Trade**, where, for the past 12 years, he has traded options on U.S. Treasury Bond and Agricultural Futures. Also, for the past three years, he has returned to his educator roots, by writing and implementing an options trading class for aspiring future's options traders.

Author's Note:

"Education is an essential ingredient for trader success." As President of **UOT Financial Services**, and founder of the **University of Trading**. I want you to know about the additional resources available to you if you decide to consider a career as a trader. The**University of Trading** (http:Universityoftrading.com) offers seminars and courses that can answer any questions concerning your futures and options floor and screen trading experience.

UOT Financial Services will assist you in becoming a trader in Chicago at the **Chicago Mercantile Exchange**, and **Chicago Board of Trade**. Software is available for a trader to use to monitor daily trading performance as well as enable a trader to identify favorable and unfavorable trading tendencies. You may contact Mickey Hoffman by telephone 312-382-1982, or EMAIL uot@earthlink.net.

TABLE OF CONTENTS

SECTION I

ON YOUR MARK

Before one begins any new journey, a number of basic preparations must take place. The same is true when one faces the arduous task of determining one's suitability for the profession of trading. An initial list of concerns must be addressed in order to determine if the individual will be able to compete in the trading game. In this first section of our discussion, we endeavor to answer the basic questions that all potential traders have, regarding the requisites of the business. *How much capital will it take to start a career in trading? If I can't finance my own career, how do I become a trader? Do I need to be a college graduate to trade? Are there courses that can teach me how to trade?* In this initial section, to get you started on your way, we will try to answer all of your questions about becoming a trader.

CAPITAL

The first and foremost question asked by a candidate for trading: *How much will it cost to launch my trading career?* Before you are allowed to set foot in a trading pit, you will have to guarantee to an exchange your ability to finance your daily trades. You do this by insuring the integrity of your trading account with cash. In other words, you will be asked to keep a certain amount of money available in an account, to cover any losses you might incur.

To be honest, it is impossible to give an exact dollar amount as each exchange has its own capital requirements. But, generally speaking, most exchanges and their member firms require enough capital in reserve to cover losses of at least five figures.

Along with the cost of guaranteeing the solvency of your trading account, you will have to include the cost of membership. All exchanges require a thorough application process, containing background checks for credit rating, security purposes and prior criminal activity. The entire process is quite expensive and the cost is paid entirely by the applicant. Again, varying from one exchange to another, this expenditure may run as high as a couple of thousand dollars or more.

In addition to processing your application for membership and guaranteeing your trading account, you will need to factor in other costs. Specifically, you will have to pay a monthly membership (seat) rental fee or else purchase a membership. Along with this initial trading overhead, you must provide for monthly living expenses. By setting aside a cash reserve, you will be able to cover all expenses until you get acclimated to your new profession. As with most new endeavors, it takes time to start showing a profit. Therefore, you should set aside a fair sum of money —anywhere from a twelve to eighteen month reserve —until you can support yourself through trading profits.

HOW DO I BECOME A TRADER?

At this point, you may be thinking that it is not financially possible to begin a trading career, due to lack of funds. However, this does not mean that the trading profession is out of the question. If you cannot personally raise the initial amount of capital needed to begin trading, be assured that there are other avenues you may pursue to reach your ultimate goal. The important point on which to focus is your goal: ***becoming a professional trader.***

If you are willing to make sacrifices to obtain your goals, there are ways to circumvent the need for a large, lump sum of capital to begin your career. The sacrifice may take the form of an entry-level position at one of the exchanges. In fact, many traders have begun their journey by working for an exchange in some capacity. This has afforded them the opportunity to learn about the business firsthand, experience the environment, and earn an income in the process. Contact the personnel office of a specific exchange to determine availability of employment. (See the end of Section I for a list of exchange possibilities and their individual addresses.)

Another path to a trading career is employment with one of the member firms that make up the body of an exchange. These firms, comprised of brokerage houses, banks, and other financial institutions, own exchange memberships that enable them to execute their customers' orders directly in the pits. Being in the employ of a large, well-capitalized member firm has definite advantages. By working for one of these firms, a potential trader gains exposure to the reality of trading. This experience may ultimately lead to the realization of your goal to become a trader. (Most exchanges will provide a list containing pertinent information regarding member firms.)

Finally, there are trading groups and individuals that actively seek potential traders. You may have to begin your career in a support position. From this initial starting point, you may work your way into becoming a candidate for a trading membership. Although the time frame for advancement will vary according to a number of factors, an individual in this employment agreement usually has a six-month to three-year apprenticeship. However, in most cases, these candidates are trained and sponsored to become trading employees. In return, the new trader is usually paid a salary, while participating in a percentage of the profits. Any financial concessions are offset through the accumulation of valuable experience, either in the trading pit or in another trading venue, such as an off the floor trading room.

How does one become acquainted with such an opportunity? Our best advice is to try any means possible to network yourself into this type of situation. This may mean that you have to take exchange sponsored educational courses, visit known after-hour haunts of traders, or go firm to firm with resume in hand, all with the expressed intent of becoming a known personality with aspirations of entering the trading fraternity. You must remember that almost all entry-level positions will be extremely low paying. However, the acceptance of this type of job will be taken as an outward indication of your dedication to achieve your goal. Your bottom line is a trade of long hours, sustained effort, and lack of pay for the eventual opportunity of trading as a career.

It is definitely to your advantage, if you cannot finance a trading debut on your own, to seek employment with the exchanges, member firms, or anyone else directly engaged in the profession of trading.

DO I NEED A COLLEGE DEGREE?

Another question that usually arises from prospective traders is one concerning the need for a college degree. At this time, to our knowledge, there is not an exchange college degree requirement. The general membership process for most exchanges examines your personal history, along with your financial ability to maintain a trading account. In addition, all exchanges require applicants to pass a test, covering rules, regulations, and relevant contract specifications.

Some people believe that a trader with a college degree has a better chance to survive the rigors of trading than someone without one. We believe this is an argument to be waged on an individual, case by case basis. On the other hand, there does seem to be some correlation between the acquisition of a degree and success in trading. This conclusion is, by no means, arrived at scientifically; however, through our personal observation, there seems to be a higher percentage of college graduates in the business than those without a degree. It must be stated, of course, that being degreed does not assure success. However, we do believe that someone who has persevered the trials and tribulations of college is afforded an edge in performance over someone who has not experienced the process.

ARE THEIR COURSES TO LEARN TRADING?

As with almost anything in this world, from woodworking to accounting to psychic awareness, there are classes offered that promise to unlock the innermost workings of any given discipline. The same is true for trading. Yes, there are classes devoted specifically to teaching the process of trading, both on and off the floor. For our purposes, we will use our own trading course as an example of available instruction for the prospective trader.

Offered in Chicago, *Pit Trading 101* and its accompanying seminars is an innovative course, designed with the novice trader in mind. Broken down into an introductory seminar and three successive courses, *Pit Trading 101* covers all aspects of the trading experience. The entire process culminates in a multi-level trading environment that simulates trading as closely as is humanly possible.

The curriculum is designed to take a potential trader through every step of the trading process, allowing an individual to experience both the physical rigors and psychological stresses. The design of the seminar, and each ensuing course, is comprehensive in nature, with the overall result being one of complete preparation for entrance into futures trading environment.

In summary, if you cannot capitalize your own entrance into the business of trading, there are a number of different ways to gain admission. In addition, there are educational courses available, designed specifically to enable a new trader to learn his chosen profession. (Both universities and colleges across the United States offer specific courses on futures and option trading; some specific institutions of higher learning even offer complete curricula designed with a degree and trading career in mind.) Remember that trading is not only for the elite or those who have the ability to bankroll themselves as a neophyte trader. This exciting occupation is open to anyone who has the initiative to work hard, the willingness to sacrifice, the patience to start at the bottom, and the perseverance to work his way to the top.

WHAT ARE MY CHOICES?

The following is a list of exchanges and information about the requirements for membership. Since the price of memberships continually changes, we have made an indication concerning cost. Memberships are rated in terms of cost with the following legend, and are by no means intended to be comprehensive:

$	= Least expensive
$$	= Moderately expensive
$$$	= Expensive
$$$$	= Very expensive

(The following commodity exchanges are listed alphabetically, with no inference of importance intended. All leases are expressed in a yearly total.)

CHICAGO BOARD OF TRADE

Memberships

Full Board of Trade Membership (Full Trading Privileges)
    Buy: $$$$
    Lease: $$$

Associate Board of Trade Membership (AM)
    Buy: $$$
    Lease: $$$

Commodity Option Membership (COM)
    Buy: $$
    Lease: $

IDEM Membership
    Buy: $
    Lease: $

Financial Requirements

There is an $1100 application fee for all new traders. The exchange does not require traders to have a minimum net worth. Individual clearing houses may decide to set financial requirements that vary from firm to firm.

Educational Requirements

All new members must attend a new member seminar and pass a written exam. No other education is required.

> *Exchange Contact*
> Joyce Blau
> 141 W. Jackson Room A10
> Chicago, IL 60604
> (312) 435-3500

CHICAGO MERCANTILE EXCHANGE

Memberships

CME (Chicago Mercantile Exchange)
Buy: $$$$
Lease: $$

IMM (International Monetary Market)
Buy: $$$
Lease: $$

IOM (Index and Options Market)
Buy: $$
Lease: $$

GEM (Growth and Emerging Markets)
Buy: $
Lease: $

Educational requirements

All traders must attend a four-hour ethics-training course.

Financial Requirements

For Gem Memberships, the capital requirement is $25K: for all other memberships $50K. All new members are required to pay an application fee of $1500.

Exchange Contact

Nancy Wendt
Membership Department
30 S. Wacker Drive
Chicago, IL 60604
(312) 930-1000

COFFEE, SUGAR, AND COCOA EXCHANGE

Memberships

Buy: $$$
Lease: $$

Associate Membership

Buy: $
Lease: $

Educational Requirements

All brokers are required to take trading classes, pass a written exam, and participate in mock trading.

Financial Requirements

The exchange does not have a set minimum net worth for traders. All traders are required to have a Clearing Member Guarantee. Individual member firms may ask for varying degrees of financial requirements, anywhere from $25K and up. All new members are required to pay $750 in application fees and $1000 in investigation fees.

Exchange Contact
Helene Recco
4 World Trade Center, 8ᵗʰ Floor
New York, NY 10048
(212) 742-6000

KANSAS CITY BOARD OF TRADE

Memberships

Class A Membership (Full Shareholder)
    Buy: $
    Lease: $*

Class B Membership (Stock Index)
    Buy: $
    Lease: $

Educational Requirements

All new members must attend a two-hour orientation course.

Financial Requirements

The exchange requires that a trader must have a net worth of $25,000. However, this standard is flexible and traders have been given floor access with a lesser amount. There is a $500 transfer fee and a $300 investigation fee required of all new members.

Exchange Contact
Kathleen Garcia
5800 Main St., Suite 303
Kansas City, MO 64112
816-931-4660

MIDAMERICA COMMODITY EXCHANGE

Memberships

Standard Trading Seat
    Buy $
    Lease   N/A

Educational Requirements

All traders must attend a new member seminar.

Financial Requirements

There is no minimum net worth required of traders. Individual trading firms may decide to require a specific net worth before allowing entry to the exchange. All members pay quarterly dues of $300. The dues may be waived if a trader executes more than 300 contracts in a quarter. There is also a $1100 application fee.

Exchange Contact
Chuck Rondini
Chicago Board of Trade
141 W. Jackson, Room A10
Chicago, IL 60604
(312) 341-3000

MINNEAPOLIS GRAIN EXCHANGE

Memberships

Standard Trading Seat
Buy $
Lease: $

Educational Requirements

There is no minimum net worth requirement. A trader is required to trade his/her own account for a minimum of three months. All new members are required to pay a $400 application fee and a $500 deposit on any lease agreement.

Exchange Contact
Jenny Hendrix
400 South 4th St., Suite 130
Minneapolis, MN 55415
(612) 321-7101

MONTREAL EXCHANGE

Memberships

Regular Memberships
Buy:	$$
Lease:	N/A

Restricted Permit (Futures Trading Only)
Buy:	$ per year for Individual traders*
Lease:	$ per year for Brokers*

*Incentive programs allow both traders and brokers to waive their fees if they trade a specific number of contracts per day.

Educational Requirements

All traders must pass specific trading courses offered by the exchange.

Financial Requirements

A $25,000 net worth (Canadian dollars) is required of all traders before they are permitted membership. Also $5000 (Canadian dollars) is required to obtain a trading permit for all traders who are not Canadian citizens.

Exchange Contact
Richard Bourbonnaire
P.O. Box 61
800 Victorian Square
Montreal, Quebec H4 1A9
(514) 871-3585

NEW YORK COTTON EXCHANGE

Memberships

Full Membership
Buy:	$$

Lease: $

Finex Membership (Non Futures Trading)
    Buy: $
    Lease: $

Educational Requirements
None

Financial Requirements

Traders are required to have a net worth of $20,000. There is also a $1000 initiation fee for all traders.

Exchange Contact
Connie Mackenzie
4 World Trade Center, 8th floor
New York, NY 10048
(212)742-5054

NEW YORK FUTURES EXCHANGE

Memberships

Standard Membership
    Buy: $
    Lease: N/A

Educational Requirements

None

Financial Requirements

Traders are required to have a net worth of $20,000. There is also a $500 application fee for all new traders.

Exchange Contact
Connie Mackenzie

4 World Trade Center, 8ᵗʰ Floor
New York, NY 10048
(212) 742-5054

NEW YORK MERCANTILE EXCHANGE

Memberships

COMEX Membership
Buy:	$$
Lease:	$

NYMEX Membership
Buy:	$$$$
Lease:	$$

Educational Requirements

New members are required to attend standard orientation courses offered by the exchange.

Financial Requirements

All traders are required to have a minimum net worth of $50,000. All new members are required to pay application fees of $700.

+Exchange Contact
Roxanne Costa
4th Floor
1 North End Avenue
New York, NY 10282
(212)630-1000

WINNEPEG COMMODITY EXCHANGE

Memberships

Standard Trading Seat
Buy:	$ (Canadian dollars)
Lease:	N/A

Educational Requirements

All traders must pass a floor trader qualification course.

Financial Requirements

Traders are required to have a minimum net worth of $20,000 (Canadian). All members must also pay annual dues of $500 (Canadian).

Exchange Contact
Carol Klopko, Corporate Secretary
360 Main Street, Suite 500
Winnepeg, Manitoba R3C 3Z4
(204)925-5000

SECTION II
Is a Career in Trading for Me?

Chapter I
The Allure of Trading

Everyone has reasons for the things they do. Which of the following categories best describes your "real" motivation for pursuing a career in trading?

Category I..........I WANT MONEY, MONEY, AND MORE MONEY!

Trading is a quick way to amass a fortune. Making a lot of money is vital to my happiness and trading is the perfect way to attain my goal of being wealthy. All traders make a lot of money, live in the most exclusive neighborhoods, own the biggest and most beautiful houses, drive the fanciest cars, travel to the most exotic places. They wear the finest clothes and most expensive jewelry, eat at the most popular restaurants, and finally, enjoy the best that life has to offer.

Category II.........I'M A COMMODITIES TRADER, IT'S THE NEXT BEST THING TO BEING A ROCK STAR!

If what you do for a living can help to define whom you are, being a commodities trader makes a bold, emphatic statement. Professional athletes, Hollywood movie actors and financial tycoons are all people admired by society. Becoming a commodity trader is a step toward the fame I so richly deserve. Once I have established myself as a premier trader, I can join the elite and live the life I have always dreamed about living.

Category III.........I WANT TO BE PART OF THE *IN CROWD* AND THE EXCITEMENT IN THE TRADING PROFESSION!

I think it would be exciting to wave my hands in the air while yelling, writing on trading cards, and wearing the colors of the professional trader. Each day, visitors from all over the world will come to observe and marvel at my ability to survive in this world of chaos called trading. I feel that being part of the process of trading and its accompanying excitement would be a perfect place to make a living, for the few, short hours a day that the exchange is open.

As you may already realize, all of the assumptions in the three categories are, to some extent, actually true. However, these presumptions do not immediately follow your admission into the trading fraternity. It is important, at this point in our journey, that we make one admission about the trading profession very clear to the reader: **TRADING IS VERY HARD WORK!** This idea will integrate itself throughout this discussion, no matter which aspect of the business we are examining. After a while, you may even think that we are over emphasizing this point, but nothing could be further from the truth. Before we get into any in-depth discussion, the reader must enter the arena armed with the knowledge that this seemingly glamorous profession is based on the same foundation as any other successful endeavor —*the sweat of one's brow*. If this inescapable point is clear to you, then continue your quest for information about the business of trading, without the illusions that most people have concerning this highly visible, fast moving profession.

SELF-HONESTY IS IMPORTANT

Your decision to become a trader must be based on factual information. While reading our book, you will discover that trading is mentally and physically demanding, as well as an emotionally draining experience. You will find that you must train extensively, conduct rigorous preparation, and have solid research in your command to be prepared to set foot on an exchange floor. In short, we will strip away the veneer of glamour mistakenly attributed to this profession. You will come to realize that it takes a lot of plain, hard work to earn the honor of wearing the loudly colored trading jacket and experience all of the glitter that accompanies a membership in one of America's fastest, most exciting industries.

As we begin our journey, we are trying to be as honest with you, our prospective trader, as we hope you are being with yourself. Do not consider trading as a career for the wrong reasons: *it is an easy way to become a millionaire, it is prestigious to tell people you are a trader* or *it looks exciting and glamorous.* Bottom line, trading should be pursued as a profession only if your inner being is consistent with the endeavor. In order to trade, you must love what you do.

Chapter II
The Positive Aspects of Trading

Only you, as an individual, can answer why you follow a particular path in life. Everyone has his own reasons for his actions, and choosing a professional career path is a highly personal decision based on one's perceived individual strengths and weaknesses and how we fit into society. This self-image narrows the selection of choices we consider possible in order to reach our goals. Someone who has poor hand-eye coordination should not aspire to become a professional baseball player any more than someone who is uncomfortable in front of large groups should attempt to become a stage performer.

In this chapter, we look at the positive aspects of trading, allowing you to take the first step in determining whether trading can be a viable career for you.

THE POSITIVES

First of all, why would anyone want to choose such a seemingly chaotic way of earning a living? From all appearances, trading in the pits seems like a jumble of waving and screaming without discernable meaning, although nothing could be further from the truth. What are the reasons someone would want to engage in this choreographed mayhem? Here are just a few examples of the positive aspects of trading:

Your Own Boss

If you become an independent trader, you are virtually the owner of your own company, consisting of a work force of one. You are the president and chief executive, making all major decisions regarding the future of your financial venture. You, and you alone, determine what course to follow, without the hassle of corporate politics and account-ability to shareholders. Although a rigorous work ethic is the norm for the independent trader, you can decide whether or not to trade and when. In short, you are the master of your own destiny.

Along with the ability to call all of your own shots comes a sense of freedom – freedom to work when you want and as long as you want. You have the option to take a vacation, if and when you feel the need, without answering to anyone about its timing or duration. As your own boss, you are in charge of every aspect of your career, making every decision about every matter that arises.

So, not only does this form of self-employment give you financial free-dom, it also affords you the ability to take charge of every aspect of your working life, while being accountable to no one.

Unlimited Financial Opportunity

Unlike a job in the regular work force, the independent trader is not bound by the restrictions of a yearly salary, hoping against hope that the potential bonus you have been promised lives up to expectations.

The independent trader, making all of the decisions affecting the finan-cial rewards of trading, has an unlimited opportunity to earn as much money as he is capable of earning. When discussing trading's unlimited financial rewards, however, it is very important to remember that these rewards come only to those individuals who are willing to put forth the effort of continuous hard work and the preparation necessary to suc-ceed, for success in trading is an arduous task. But, unlike most other professions where other factors may hinder success, in trading, your bottom line realistically reflects how good you really are.

Excitement, Exhilaration, and Ride of a Lifetime

The one thing a professional trading career can guarantee is excitement. There is no other place in the business world that can generate the excitement and exhilaration one feels while standing in the pit, waiting for the opening bell to begin trading. Each day, the unpredictable awaits you, as you ready yourself for the ride of your life.

There is something to be said about the actual process of trading, too. The very essence of trading is a stimulating and challenging experience, since you make the decisions and reap the rewards or suffer the consequences. However, it is sometimes the very process of trading that can sweep you up and catch you in its alluring grasp. Trading can become an end in itself. It is hard to describe accurately to someone who has never traded, the type of feeling experienced by a trader when he succeeds in the face of what seems to be, at times, insurmountable odds. In such instances, you feel as though you can take on the whole world. As difficult as it is to succeed in such a competitive, every-man-for-himself business, there is no greater satisfaction than the knowledge that you have beaten the game on its own terms. In many instances, you may not even show a profit, but the effort to snatch victory from the jaws of defeat just to break even, can sometimes seem reward enough.

At the sound of the closing bell, no matter what the financial outcome of the day, few other careers can weave a magic spell the way trading can, challenging the trader to return for another day's battle. Unlike many professions where boredom can become the norm, being a trader is a unique experience where each day is unlike the preceding one, opening a wealth of possibilities for self-discovery and personal growth.

Learn Who You Really Are

One of the things that most people do not realize is that trading affords more than just a way of making a comfortable living. Like Sir Edmund Hillary's assault upon Mt. Everest or Thor Heyerdahl's adventures aboard his raft, the Kon Tiki, there is more than just the obvious financial result from an attempt to perform an extremely difficult task. In both cases, for these two world-renowned adventurers, the accolades of accomplishment were also accompanied by a measure of self-realization.

Trading affords the same introspection for the trader that Hillary's attempt to conquer the world's highest peak or Heyerdahl's reenactment of the voyages of the Polynesians of the Pacific did for the individuals involved in these record setting endeavors. Since you are solely dependent upon yourself and your abilities, you will quickly discover who and what you really are. As a trader, one experiences the emotional highs and lows resulting from the euphoria of success and the depression of failure. You will confront your inner demons and be forced to transcend their influence. Through the tests of adversity a trader normally endures, you will quickly come to understand that which makes you uniquely you. In a revealing sense, trading not only becomes a vehicle to financial security, it also becomes a test of an individual and his inner being.

Time Flexibility

There are a number of other positives that result from choosing trading as a profession. Some of these perks result directly from being one's own boss and some result from the intrinsic nature of the business of trading, allowing both freedom in time management as well as dress.

Because you are your own boss, you may come and go as you please. This may sound like a somewhat trivial matter, but, due to the stressful nature of trading (which will be discussed later in the text), it is important to be able to take advantage of this particular aspect of freedom that trading affords. This freedom pertains not only to the scheduling of vacation time, but also to the daily grind one must survive. Having the opportunity to leave the trading floor and assess the situation in detail is a valuable luxury.

Taking the idea of flexible time and freedom a step further, some traders actually set individual daily goals for themselves regarding the amount of money they need to earn. If and when they reach their desired amount in any one given day, some choose to leave the trading pit, to insure keeping what they earned. There are few, if any, other business that afford the individual the opportunity to set a goal, reach it, and then go home. Again, this luxury comes from the very basic nature of trading and being one's own boss. If you want to earn **x** amount of dollars and stop, no one can tell you otherwise, nor can they force you to remain in the pit.

In addition to flexible scheduling, the working hours for most pit traders are much shorter than traditional, corporate working hours. The shorter workday is a result of the intrinsic nature of the business and the pressure the individual trader must endure during the course of a normal day. Since each moment of a trader's working time is filled with a myriad of details and difficult decisions, the daily regimen of a pit trader is designed to be short, allowing adequate time for regeneration between trading sessions.

Pit Politics

The nature of the trading pit allows for a measure of honesty not found in the boardrooms of business. Trading is a fast-paced, every-man-for-himself environment, where there isn't time for social amenities; confrontations are always out in the open and no verbal punches are pulled during disagreements. However, with the absence of politics in the conventional sense, where favoritism precedes financial advancement, your expertise as a trader, not your skill at amassing political allies and winning favor, will chart your rise to success. Of course, all trading is not performed in a vacuum, so some measure of social and political skill are necessary, as would be the case in any situation where diverse individuals are brought together. Therefore, it is you and your ability to trade successfully that will always win over any obstacles you encounter, political or otherwise.

SUMMARY

In summation, the positive aspects of trading are fulfilling both financially as well as personally. Being an entrepreneur and owning your own business affords great opportunity for personal growth and creativity. Unlike a corporate position, the factor of unlimited financial opportunity can inspire you to perform to the best of your ability, while being amply compensated commensurate to your efforts. Faced with the possibility of a unique work environment, where anything may happen, your everyday existence becomes more meaningful and exciting. Through the trials and tribulations of this unusual day to day existence, you will have an opportunity to examine and comprehend yourself and your performance. With the flexibility that trading affords, you can determine your own schedule of time and activities to correlate to your personal needs.

Finally, unlike the corporate world where your destiny may be determined by someone else, without your input, trading affords you the opportunity to create your own future.

Chapter III
The Negative Aspects of Trading

From examining the positive aspects of trading, you would think that everyone would endeavor to become a part of the business, since its intrinsic nature is one of freedom —both financially and personally. Unfortunately, there is also a debit side in the ledger book of trading, containing some major, but not insurmountable obstacles to success. Some of the negatives are addressed in this chapter.

THE NEGATIVES

You Are Your Own Boss

Being one's own boss is a positive aspect of trading because it offers freedom and flexibility. However, for some individuals who lack the discipline to work on their own, this very fact is a considerable negative. Problems usually arise when a person who lacks the discipline provided by a solid work ethic acts as his own boss. Many times, an undisciplined trader will suffer from excessive absence and uninspired performance since no one is there to supervise and correct negative habits when they arise. Trading is not for those who must be watched carefully to insure completion of a task; trading is for independent individuals who can stand on their own, make decisions without consultation, and are ready to accept the consequences of their decisions. In other work situations, it may be possible to deflect blame elsewhere if things go awry; when one chooses to trade and be responsible for the bottom line, the success or failure of each day resides squarely on the shoulder of the independent trader. To be a successful trader, you have to be the type of person who can perform to the best of your ability without the need of constant supervision.

The Other Side of Unlimited Opportunity

One of the positive aspects of trading is that you have unlimited opportunity. On the other side of the trading ledger, there may be days when you work hard to succeed, but do not. When in the employ of others, you may not always present your best effort, but you are ensured of a paycheck; as a trader who owns his own business, there will be times when you struggle for days, weeks, or even months, without gaining financial ground. The fact of the matter is that you can go to work all day, work until you are exhausted, and not only end up with no financial gain, but also suffer financial losses that are emotionally destructive and potentially career ending. You must be cognizant of this possibility and prepared for it at all times.

You Are the Decision Maker

Trading involves making decisions under unparalleled pressure. If a trader is disciplined, he will be successful, because he will stick to a preconceived game plan—a set of rules that tell him how much risk to take and when to take a profit or suffer a loss. Staying within a prescribed set of rules of performance keeps one out of trouble. But, a trader who lacks the discipline to stay within the rules may not want to face a situation where it is tough to make a decision, especially when it comes time to take a financial loss. For certain personality types, dealing with adversity is not only difficult, it is nearly impossible. If the inability to make difficult decisions and perform under pressure manifests itself, the results can be catastrophic. If you are a person who does not embrace decision-making and the challenge it presents, then trading will not be a viable career.

Pressure, Stress and Ultimate Burnout

As with any type of work, trading has a measure of stress attached to it. The stress results from the pressure of the job.

The prospective trader must understand the basic nature of the trading, all of which unfolds in the most adversarial of environments— the trading pit. Traders are squeezed together, trying to get the best possible prices for their trades. People are pushing, shoving, yelling, and vying for position, all the while concerned only for themselves and their own success and survival. Add to this equation that each moment brings more information to ingest and more decisions to make. You can readily begin to understand the pressure packed situation a trader must face each and every trading day of his career.

When you also add the fact that there is no guarantee of financial security in the form of a paycheck and the possibility of suffering large monetary losses, the stress involved in the job is apparent. Earlier we pointed out that the rewards of trading are many, but if you examine the nature of trading, you can understand how traders may suffer from the pressure of having to make decision after decision, each resulting in financial gain or loss. From the daily pressure to make the right decisions, stress builds.

Unfortunately, the pressure packed scenario of assimilating, ingesting and evaluating information continues, day after day, in the life of a trader. Successful traders learn to cope with the basic pressure of the job. In order to be successful, one must learn to dissipate the stressful aspects of trading; however, if you do not learn to cope or are unable to recognize the toll the stress of trading can bring upon you, the result can be trader burnout.

Burnout is that state of mind that overtakes a trader and incapacitates him, preventing him from performing his function in the pit to the best of his ability. Many times, traders suffering from burnout stand around, unable to make the decisions that are necessary during the course of a normal business day. Burnout causes the individual trader to question whether or not to make a particular trade, rather than react to it. When this type of behavior occurs, the best thing a trader can do is take time out to regroup. No matter how successful the trader, burnout is always a possibility and it must be recognized as a negative aspect of trading that needs attention.

Keeping up with the Jones'

This well-known syndrome is the one in which a person tries to equal or better the successes of his friends or neighbors. This is usually accomplished by purchasing larger or more expensive versions of the commonly recognized symbols of success. These purchases are made in order to display to others one's rightful stature in the financial hierarchy of life. However, when related to trading, this syndrome takes on an additional life, for not only does it apply to the purchase of fancier automobiles and larger, more expensive homes, but it also manifests itself in the trading pit through a change in behavior.

Many times, this need to prove oneself in the eyes of others changes the way a trader operates. This change in behavior causes the individual to take on more risk than is comfortable in order to earn the additional money to pay for these newly desired "toys" of success. This need to display one's personal worth through acquisitions causes a trader to risk more to earn more. The added risk also brings the added possibility of larger losses. If the motivation to show off to others is accompanied by a change in behavior, the result is usually a negative one. Changes in trading style and the number of contracts normally traded must flow in a natural progression. Positive changes do not occur artificially, especially when instituted by a need to show others how successful you are.

A rush to greater financial rewards must be accompanied by experience, followed by incremental development, additional work, and the increased preparation necessary to attain those rewards, not by a need to pay for new acquisitions. Unlike the sentiment expressed by Gordon Gekko, the unscrupulous stock manipulator portrayed so well by Michael Douglas in the movie, *Wall Street,* who said *"sometimes, greed is good,"* in this case it is **NOT** good. When you are motivated by a need to make more money to impress friends and relatives, you have succumbed to the negative motivation commonly known as *The Jones Complex.*

The Trader's Complex

For most people who know little about the business, this is easily the greatest misconception regarding trading: all traders are millionaires. For the new trader, it is easy to be misled into thinking that everyone else in the pit is making a great deal of money, and since you are now part of the trading brotherhood, you too will be making big bucks in record time. This misconception almost always leads to disaster because appearances are often deceiving. Trading is not as simplistic as it seems. Certainly, wanting to succeed is a positive goal; however, wanting to make it big without the hard work and "dues paying" that are necessary to succeed is a common pitfall of the new trader. As long as you understand that trading is hard work, you will stand on steady ground; regard trading as an easy way to make big dough and you will be sinking in the quicksand of failure before you realize what is happening to you.

Noise and More Noise

When people see a trading floor for the first time, the one thing that seems to stand out the most is the **NOISE**. Traders are yelling while waving their arms and hands amid a symphony of activity that usually causes the observer to wonder how anyone can make any sense of it all. For the potential trader, this element of constant activity, accompanied by the accentuated noise level must be considered, when making an intelligent decision about a trading future.

If you are a person who is energized by activity around you, then this aspect of trading will be a positive influence on your performance; however, if you are unnerved by the distraction of movement and noise, then trading could be an impossible endeavor. The difficult part about this unique aspect of trading is that not many other workplaces offer a person the opportunity to discover whether or not noise will be a hindering factor in performance. With the exception of professional athletes who perform before cheering crowds, most people work in places where noise is a minimal influence.

Shoulder to Shoulder

If you have ever watched a trading pit, you may have noticed that the traders were all bunched together, shoulder to shoulder, moving and swaying as a singular organism. This phenomenon occurs because trading is an open out-cry system that causes traders to gather around the sources of the trading orders. By being in close proximity to a floor broker, a trader has a better chance of being recognized as the first respondent to a broker's request for a bid to buy or an offer to sell a contract. What one must realize, when observing the pit, is that, in order to trade for a living, one must be able to deal with others working in close, physical proximity, all day long.

If you are someone who gets uncomfortable in crowded elevators or when someone is standing close to you, then trading will be a difficult undertaking; and in conjunction with the actual tight quarters involved in the trading pit, one must recognize the fact that you will be standing, moving around in those tight quarters, yelling and waving to be recognized, and in general, operating in difficult physical surroundings, for extended periods of time. In short, trading is a physical endeavor that taxes both the mind and body. In order to succeed, you must be able to operate in this environment that does not lend itself to solitude or personal comfort.

The Fear of Making Mistakes

For most of us, during the course of a workday, each individual task performed is not accompanied with the fear that a particular decision may end employment. Sure, most of us worry about job security, but not with each and every thing we do.

Trading, however, does allow for a certain amount of fear to be attached to one's performance during each day's normal events.

No one, no matter how great a trader, can have a winner with each trade executed. All experienced traders realize that each day will bring a number of winning trades and a number of losing trades; simply put, the object of trading is to out-pace the losers with winners.

So, when someone looks at trading with the intention of making it an occupation, one must examine there ability to deal with failure as well as success. Trading is a complicated combination of both success and failure. If you have an inherent fear of making mistakes, then trading is not for you. Fear has a way of incapacitating people, freezing them in their tracks, and preventing them from performing. If the fear of making a mistake overtakes you, it can render you totally ineffective. Robbed of the ability to act when the opportunity arises because he is afraid of making a mistake, the trader cannot take advantage of the moment, his sole purpose in the trading pit.

Taking the fear factor a step further, if a trader has executed a trade that becomes a losing one, fear may incapacitate him to the point where he cannot act aggressively to limit his losses. When a pit trader stands around, waiting and hoping that his losing trade will turn around and become a winning one, he has lost the battle. Instead of acting, accepting the loss and preparing himself for the next opportunity to make money, this trader has frozen himself into an ineffective member of the pit, becoming a spectator rather than a participant.

You Are All Alone!

The basic nature of trading calls upon the individual to work alone, competing with everyone else in the pit to succeed. Without the support system present, or a teamwork situation to bolster an individuals confidence in the face of difficult situations, a trader must be confident on his own. Therefore, since you, solely, are making decision after decision without assistance, you and you alone may be accountable for your performance. Some individuals are uncomfortable being sole proprietors, depending exclusively on one's self to succeed.

As in all things in life, it is the manner one learns to manage adversity that is important. Different people deal with adversity in different ways. For the prospective trader, a thorough examination of how he would realistically deal with the negative aspects of trading must be honestly considered before making a decision to become a trader. Our object in this chapter has been to present the important aspects as honestly and forthrightly as possible and let you assess you ability to deal with them.

SECTION III
The Anatomy of a Market

Chapter I
Market Basics:
The Elevator Analogy

Previously, we presented information to help you determine if the business of trading is right for you. Since we have peaked your interest, it may now be helpful to give you a basic example of how a market works. The following is a simple, yet concise presentation of the basics of market movement. If you are not familiar with how a market works, this should help you understand the process.

[Note: For those of you who are familiar with markets and how they operate, be they financial, commodity, or security, at this point, you may want to skip to the next chapter.]

To make sure we are all beginning from square one, let's examine the market and how it works. Traders exist to buy and sell contracts in the market. No matter what is being traded in a pit, you should have a comprehensive understanding of how a market works, before you attempt to make a decision about whether or not you would like to trade for a living.

Making a very simple analogy, a market can be compared to an elevator. Just as an elevator goes up and down, so does the price for a share of a company's stock, a pork belly, or bushel of corn. If more people want to buy than sell, the price rises; when more people want to sell than buy, the price goes down. The whole process is that simple.

For our purposes, let's imagine you are an elevator commodity trader, sitting at a computer screen. On the screen, there is a representation of an elevator which has the ability to go up or down, at any given time. On the top of the elevator is a number, representing the floor on which the elevator is stopped. For example if the elevator is on the 30th floor and you anticipate it going up to the 31st floor, then you push the blue button for one ticket with the number 30 on it. If the elevator does indeed proceed to the 31st floor, you may now reverse the process, by pressing the red button that allows you to sell one ticket with the number 31 on it. A blue ticket to buy, with a lower number (30), and a red ticket to sell, with a higher number (31), means that you have correctly predicted the direction of the elevator. For each floor, there is the possibility of a profit of ten dollars for one ticket. Therefore, since your first prediction or trade was correct, you have earned ten dollars. Had you waited until the elevator stopped on the 32nd floor, you would have realized a profit of ten dollars more, a total of twenty dollars, and so on, for each floor above.

To summarize, you thought that the elevator was going up. You bought a blue ticket denoting a rise of the elevator, from the 30th floor. The elevator went to the 31st floor, making your prediction correct. You then offset your one blue ticket buy, on floor 30, with one red ticket sell, on floor 31. You make a profit of ten dollars for a correct prediction of a one-floor move with one ticket.

When you are ready to make your next trade, you find that the elevator is now stopped on floor 39. Your prediction is that the elevator will descend to the 38th floor. If you examine the order of events from your first trade, when you predicted upward movement, you bought a blue ticket first and then sold a red ticket. The blue ticket denoted a rise of the elevator, while the red ticket completed the process. In this instance, with the prediction of downward movement, you must reverse the order, by selling a red ticket with the number 39 on it first. If and when the elevator goes to the 38th floor, you may then complete the transaction by buying a blue ticket with a 38 on it. Again you have predicted correctly, realizing a profit of ten dollars.

To summarize your second trade, you believed the elevator was going to go down. You needed to set up the order of events to accommodate that idea. Therefore, you reversed the order of your first trade, by selling a red ticket from the 39th floor, and then buying a blue ticket from the 38th floor. Since the red ticket (selling) had a number higher (39) than the lower (38) blue ticket (buying), you made a ten dollar profit. So, you sold on floor 39 and bought on floor 38, predicting correctly the movement of the elevator. It should be noted that, if you believe that the elevator is going down, you begin your trade by selling a red ticket to take advantage of downward movement.

A number of things must also be noted here. Every trade begins with either a buy of a contract or a sell of a contract. Then, the opposite must be executed to complete the trade. It does not matter which side starts the process; the only difference is that buying first denotes future upward movement, while selling first denotes future downward movement.

As simplistic as our elevator game appears, you must remember that there is the possibility of anticipating market movement incorrectly, too. Had you bought a blue ticket on the 30th floor and were forced to sell a red ticket when the elevator stopped on the 29th floor, predicting incorrectly, you would have lost ten dollars. Conversely, had you sold a red ticket on floor 39 and were forced to buy a blue ticket on 40, you would have lost ten dollars with that incorrect prediction.

In its simplest terms, a market is exactly like the elevator ride described here. You enter the market by purchasing or selling whatever you are trading, with the hope that it will go in the direction you have anticipated. In simple fact, traders do nothing more, but buy or sell tickets to ride the elevator of market movement, hoping that they have correctly anticipated the direction of the market.

Therefore, before you make your decision regarding trading as your chosen occupation, make sure you comprehend, on even this overly simplistic level, the reason a trader exists in the trading pit.

Chapter II
Science, Art or Just
Plain Gambling?

If, after an honest assessment of why you want to be a trader, you feel that your motivation is based on solid reasoning, we need to proceed to an analysis the basic nature of trading. Does it really make a difference if trading is a science—something that consists of preparation, research, charting, and fundamentals; or an art—something to be mastered in a creative way, or just plain gambling? How does the answer to this question affect your decision about whether or not trading is for you?

Trading is a combination of the two basic elements, science and art, without any gambling. No successful trader would even consider using only one of the two basic elements of trading without the other. Trading is a mixture, it is partially an art, a good deal of science, with a very small element of luck. Gambling should be reserved for your vacations to Las Vegas because it plays no part in the life of a professional trader. Aside from what the general public thinks about trading, traders are not gamblers. No trader "worth his salt" will enter a pit hoping to guess what will happen. Instead, a successful trader comes prepared with information of every conceivable sort, anticipating any possible scenario in the market. It takes hard work to earn money as a trader and no one is willing to give it away by gambling on what may happen. Traders search for information on which to base their decisions.

If you want to trade, and do it for any length of time, you will have to prepare yourself with all of the information science can afford you. By preparing to trade with scientific data, you are equipping yourself to succeed with the best possible odds. As we mentioned, there is also a part of trading that is an art. Art is, in this context, an intuitive sense that comes from practicing your craft and understanding its intricacies. Through practice and experience, the art of trading develops from that which is neither science nor luck. The true art of trading consists of an ability that is developed and nurtured, allowing the trader to assimilate all of the information available and evaluate it instantaneously. Traders have a name for this ability—"market feel."

In summary, trading is the perspiration of hard work, using all of the scientific data available. Along with the effort of preparation is an art of intuitive feeling that develops with time, experience, and a little bit of luck, rolled into a single storehouse of trading knowledge. Whether you develop one of the many different trading styles we will cover in another chapter, or develop one uniquely of your own makings, does not matter. In either case, you will want to incorporate both of the basic elements of trading-science and art—into your chosen strategy, to gain the greatest advantage possible.

Chapter III
The Rollercoaster and What
Makes it Move

To this point, the focus of the text has been to help you decide whether trading is a viable career for you. You have been provided with basic information suggesting possible ways to enter the business. You have also been alerted to the type of workplace in which you will be competing. Through a simple analogy in Chapter 1, the elevator trading game, you learned how a market operates.

In this chapter, we will examine the factors that influence the movement of a market. You may have questions regarding how and why markets move, such as: *Is there a way to accurately predict the direction of the market? What outside factors can cause a market to react? Do the various market players have any effect on what the market will do?* All of these questions are valid ones and their answers should become part of your overall market knowledge.

TECHNICAL FACTORS

There have been a countless number of books written with the intent of explaining exactly which technical factors are the most important. Each individual school of thought maintains that its particular focus is the primary one that accurately predicts market direction. The truth of the matter is there is no one reason a market does what it does. In each marketplace, there are a number of mitigating influences pushing and pulling the market, each with its own effect. This compilation of factors compels the market to do what it does, preventing them from becoming more important than another becomes.

There are, however, some tried and true methods that have been in use for many years, which give a good account of them when applied correctly. On its most basic level, charting an excellent way to learn about the historic ups and downs of a contract, while giving a reasonable expectation of potential future movement. Through charting, a trader marks the price movement of a contract on a graph, noting highs and lows for a specific period of time. A chart may denote price movement from minute to minute, hour to hour, day to day, etc. depending upon the needs of the user. Whatever the specifics, charting allows you to see where a commodity has traded and, through interpretation, anticipate where it may trade in the future.

Using this information, a good chartist may be able to draw intelligent conclusions about future market direction. These conclusions, drawn from chart analysis, eventually become a technical factor of their own making. If enough chartists draw the same inference from looking at a chart, that body of opinion becomes a market force in itself, putting pressure on the market to move in a specific direction. Since charting is a widely practiced discipline, it can become an independent market factor on its own. Thus, the phenomenon of a self-fulfilling technical factor is born.

There are many different types of charting. We recommend that you familiarize yourself with each type and choose one with which you feel most comfortable.

ECONOMIC FACTORS

No matter what contract you are trading, there will always be economic factors influencing the market. Whether you are trading agricultural products, financial instruments, currencies, market indices, etc., there will always be news of an economic nature that will affect the price of the contract. The following are just a few examples of the possible economic influences that can affect market movement:

FINANCIAL INSTRUMENTS – By their very name, contracts such as U.S. Treasury Bonds, Eurodollars, Foreign Currencies, and Interest Rate contracts are all heavily influenced by economic factors. You must be aware of governmental announcements, both domestic and foreign, regarding the health of the economy, the direction of interest rates, and the money supply, to keep abreast of possible market movement.

COMMODITIES – As with Financial Instruments, Commodity prices are subject to economic forces that relate directly to the individual commodity in question. For example, governmental figures regarding interest rates are less influential in determining the price of an agricultural product, such as soybeans, than are the government's crop reports predicting acres planted and crop yield. When trading commodities, you must also be aware of other economic factors such as import-export figures and weather conditions that can push prices in a particular direction.

This short overview of economic factors is a sampling of the multitude of possibilities that can influence market govement. They are not, under any circumstances, to be considered as a comprehensive list. It is recommended that you compile your own list of influential economic factors for your particular chosen contract and become familiar with all their inherent implications.

POLITICAL FACTORS

This is an area which may not immediately come to mind as part of the equation of factors that influences market movement. However, with a little thought, one can easily see how political factors could greatly affect the marketplace. Whether it is the raising of interest rates by the Federal Reserve to make the dollar look attractive, the threat of war, or the attempted assassination of the President; political factors may be instrumental in shaping the direction of a market.

INTERNATIONAL FACTORS

Markets may also be influenced by persons and events in foreign countries. If the implications are far reaching, these people or events may affect the movement of contracts traded on our American exchanges.

There are a number of incidents that come to mind that exemplify the concept of the influence of international factors on our markets: corn prices usually soar when foreign governments announce intended imports from the U.S. market, the U.S. Dollar may rise or drop sharply when foreign reserve banks announce the purchase or sale of our currency, and when the mad cow disease affected the livestock of Great Britain, our live cattle market rose to new levels in anticipation of foreign buying. All of these factors, though not directly tied to the marketplace, had an enormous impact on the direction of those markets.

MARKET PARTICIPANT FACTORS

There are two additional factors one should consider when trying to predict market movement. The first factor concerns market participants who trade large numbers of contracts. Institutional or commercial investors are market participants who trade with a great deal of capital at their disposal. Since they are powerful players, they influence market direction through their participation.

A diligent trader is always alert to the presence of powerful investors. Should the large players make their presence known, the trader with a ready game plan will have a course of action. Armed with the knowledge that a large investor is either entering or exiting the marketplace, the observant trader can then use this knowledge to his trading advantage.

Just as it is valuable to make note of the presence of large outside investors in the marketplace, it follows that the same is true when examining the influence of your fellow traders. During the course of the trading day, large volume local traders build up trading positions. It may be to your advantage to join on the same side of the market, buying when they buy and selling when they sell.

In another, quite opposite situation, if the market makes an unexpected move, trapping these large volume traders with an overabundance of contracts in the opposition of current market movement, your awareness of their positions may give you another advantage. Therefore, awareness of both large market investors and large local traders only goes to support our earlier contention that an observant trader can keep ahead of the game by remembering who is in the marketplace, and what side of the market the bulk of the players are on.

In summation, the roller coaster ride you take certainly can be anticipated through diligent preparation. Your awareness of the factors that influence the market is imperative for your continued existence as a professional trader.

Chapter IV
How Does It All Work?

They Don't Call It a Pit for Nothing

As you may already know, trading takes place inside of an area called a trading pit. If you were to examine a pit closely, you could easily draw an analogy between the trading pits of today and the arenas of the ancient Roman Empire. Existing in various shapes and sizes, all trading pits have one element in common: the pit is populated with gladiators, fighting for survival, wielding weapons of choice against their pit adversaries.

Each pit is a modern day battlefield for today's neo-gladiator. These warriors engage in a financial contest to determine who shall prevail, to claim the spoils of war —the trading profits. Striving for distinction, recognition, and wealth, the battles of the pit trader are fierce and only the elite survives to continue the quest.

Since the livelihood of the pit trader is at stake, it is necessary to be totally prepared; each and every trade has the potential to be career ending. For the gladiator to survive, he must be ready to do battle with his worthy opponents, and it is exactly the same for the pit trader, when venturing into the trading arena. It is extremely unwise to enter into a battle, if you have no plan of defense, should something unexpected confront you. Therefore, it is a well armed trader who enters the pit with knowledge —knowledge of both the market he is trading and an understanding of the players with whom he will be competing against in this marketplace.

In another chapter, we profile a number of different trading styles prevalent in the pits. At this point, a closer examination of the players who subscribe to these different trading styles will be helpful in preparing you for your journey, should you choose to attempt it.

WHO'S ON FIRST, WHAT'S ON SECOND, ETC.

In order to survive, a new trader must realize that a hierarchy exists in each and every trading pit. Although we may have given an impression to the contrary, for very good reasons, there exists a caste system, a pecking order, and a very discernible class alignment, among the members of the pit. It is beneficial for a new trader to recognize and understand this fact of trading life as soon as possible, in order to use it to his advantage. You must also understand that, in the beginning of our career, you are at the very bottom level of this hierarchy.

Earlier in the text, we stated that the only obstacles to success are those of your own making. It may now appear that, with the admission that a hierarchy exists, there are other obstacles in your path, not under your control. This class system, although it may seem unfair, was born out of purpose—market efficiency.

You may ask how this pit hierarchy promotes market efficiency. The answer to this question is found through an examination of the various members of the trading pit and where they physically stand in the pit configuration. At the very top of the pit caste system is the floor broker. A floor broker is a member who does not trade for his own account. He executes orders on behalf of various market players: brokerage houses, institutional investors, off the floor traders, etc. Usually found standing on the highest step of the trading pit to facilitate the entrance and exit of orders, floor brokers prefer to surround themselves with traders willing to trade a large number of contracts at one time. Since each order must be endorsed with the names of the traders participating, the fewer names on an order, the less chance of error.

Next in importance in the pit hierarchy is the individual pit trader known as a local. Herein lie the roots of the pit hierarchy. This evolution is brought about by the relationship between the floor broker and the individual trader. Traders want the edge, the ability to buy where the majority is buying and sell where the majority is selling. Since traders can only gain the edge by trading with the public orders in the possession of floor brokers, all traders want to stand as close as possible to the floor brokers. Proximity allows a local be heard first, when a floor broker announces an order. Also adding to the development of the pit hierarchy is the fact that floor brokers want to eliminate miscommunications during trading. Any error, when prices are changing dramatically during the course of trading can be very costly. In the language of the pit, these errors in communication are known as out-trades (trades that do not match up when compared to each other, having a difference of quantity bought or sold, price, expiration, etc.). Brokers try to surround themselves with traders who trade error-free. In conclusion, anyone who is physically near the broker gains the advantage of being first to respond. Also, it is easier to check the details of a trade when the parties involved are near each other.

The result of this evolution is a pit configuration with floor brokers, who execute a large number of orders during the course of a business day, surrounded by traders who are willing to do large numbers of contracts in one trade. This symbiotic arrangement of brokers and locals comprises the upper echelon of the pit hierarchy. Below that, are other floor brokers, who may not have as many customer orders, surrounded by traders. This configuration continues to the floor of the trading pit. At the bottom of the pit hierarchy is the new trader, trading one contract at a time, looking for a place to call home. In time, as he learns and progresses, he strives to earn the right to move to the next level or step, culminating in a place of honor on the top step of the trading pit.

Removing floor brokers and individual traders from the picture, you might be surprised to find a number of people remaining. These support personnel do not trade, but without them, trading would virtually cease. With a number of different responsibilities, each performs a function that is an integral part of the trading process. In addition to floor brokers and local traders these are the following support personnel:

ARBITRAGE CLERK – The first part of this particular individual's job is "quote the market" or disseminate information coming from the pit. Standing on the top step with his back to the pit, he quotes the market to brokerage houses, trading institutions, and any interested parties. Using hand signals, he expresses the current price where buyers are bidding and sellers are offering. With speed and accuracy, the arbitrage clerk's primary function is to relay orders from his customers to the brokers for whom he works, so that they may be executed at the current market prices. Since markets are subject to instantaneous change, the ARBITRAGE CLERK and his broker must work in consort, to get the best price possible for their customers.

BROKERS ASSISTANT – A BROKER'S ASSISTANT has the responsibility of accepting any orders arriving in the pit for his particular broker to fill on paper and placing them in an organized stack called a deck. Constantly referring to this deck, a BROKER'S ASSISTANT alerts the FLOOR BROKER to any order that is on the market, so that the broker may execute it at the right time. After a transaction has been completed, the BROKER'S ASSISTANT checks the specifics of the trade with the local, to verify all pertinent information. His job, then, is to send the order back to the firm or individual, completing the trading cycle.

TRADE CHECKER (LOCAL) – A TRADE CHECKER's job is to maintain an accurate total of the number of contracts bought and sold by his trader. This individual seeks out opposing traders and/or their trade checking assistants, to match and validate the recorded information, in order to uncover and eliminate any errors that may have resulted through miscommunication. There is also a counterpart to this individual who works for a FLOOR BROKER. His job is to check the trades executed by his Broker.

RUNNER – A RUNNER is a person who physically takes an order

written on paper, "runs" it to the trading pit for execution by the floor broker. Since a RUNNER brings the paper to the BROKER'S ASSISTANT, there often is misidentification of this individual as a member of the pit support staff. In fact, RUNNERS are support staff of brokerage firms, institutions, and exchange member firms who do business in the pit. Therefore, although seen in the vicinity of the trading pit, technically, this person is not really part of it.

PRICE REPORTER – A PRICE REPORTER is an employee of the exchange, whose job is to record current price information. Individuals on the floor of the exchange, the world's financial community, and the general public all use this information. Located on the perimeter, slightly above each pit, these reporters electronically record price changes that are then transmitted in various forms to interested parties all over the world.

To the novice, the pit looks like a jumble of humanity engaged in some sort of impenetrable activity without meaning. In reality, if you understand the function each person in that jumble is performing, you can better understand what is taking place. The pit is not random activity at a high decibel level; on the contrary, it is a simplistic set of components comprised of individuals who are brought together to work in unison for a common purpose. Each player has a predetermined role that helps to ensure an efficiently, functioning marketplace.

SECTION IV
The Anatomy of a Trader

Chapter I

YOU, YOUR COMPETITION, AND THE TRADING FLOOR

When entering any financial endeavor, one usually wants to know the odds for success. *Who or what is the greatest obstacle in my path to success? Who is my competition? How do they do what they do? Why do they do the things they do? Why should I want to join them?* In this chapter, we take a close look at the types of traders who inhabit the trading pit. Secondly, we examine the myriad of trading styles you will encounter, should you decide to enter the arena yourself. Finally, we present the most important reason to make a commitment to enter the trading pit, for anyone who wants to make a living through trading.

To dispel the myth yet another time, not everybody who trades in the pit makes a million dollars a year. On the other hand, there are traders who do make a million dollars a year, year after year, because they are the best at what they do. Whether you, too, can be one of those traders who earns a great deal of money remains to be seen, but it is not out of the question. However, the road to financial rewards is not an easy one.

Before we introduce you to the players in the trading population, let us quickly examine your main competitor —YOU! In any discussion examining those who will be your competition, you must first evaluate yourself and your willingness to persist against the difficult and trying circumstances that will confront you on a daily, weekly, monthly, and perhaps even an annual basis. It is your strength of self that will be the foundation on which to base an attack against the competition. YOU, and you alone, will determine how well you stack up in comparison to your opponents. All else aside, YOU will be the one who will have to steel yourself for the daily battle in the pits. If YOU are willing to devote the time and demonstrate the inner strength to persevere, then there will be no stopping you in your quest to succeed.

With the understanding that YOU are the single most important factor in the development of a successful trading career, let's see what else will be mitigating against your efforts for financial gains. The next factor standing between you and trading success is the competition —those traders surrounding you in the pit, vying with you to buy or sell the same commodity, financial instrument, or security you are trading. These fellow sojourners may be novices, such as yourself, but most likely are seasoned veterans, who can perform at the million-dollar level. If you observe them closely, you will see a number of different, identifiable trading styles from which you may wish to pattern your own trading persona.

THE SCALPER

The most basic trading style is SCALPING. Throughout the trading day, this short term trader buys and sells or sells and buys contracts, attempting to make small, incremental profits. The single, identifying factor for all scalpers is that they buy and sell an equal number of contracts each trading session. His profit arises when the SCALPER buys a contract at a lower price and sells it at a higher price (or sells it at a higher price and then buys it at a lower price). Every market is comprised of participants who want to either buy or sell a particular commodity. Those who want to buy the commodity have a bid (the price they are willing to pay to buy the commodity) and those who want to sell, have an offer (the price they are willing to sell the commodity). The SCALPER attempts to buy on the bid and sell on the offer, profiting on the difference in price. This bid/offer differential is the basis of the pit trader's advantage that results from the fact that he is in the pit, immediately responding to market changes. This ability to instantly adapt to market price fluctuations is the most important weapon in the SCALPER'S arsenal. Using this advantage to buy at a lower price and sell at a higher price, the SCALPER'S job is a simple one: make a profit on each trade resulting from the difference in the price which he has bought the contract to the price at which he has sold the contract. This strategy of scalping reduces trading to its basic, rudimentary form of "buy low, sell high," with few complications involved.

Under the general heading of scalper, there are a number of different techniques utilized in the scalping approach to the market. Some of the varied types of scalpers are:

1. EDGE SCALPER - the EDGE SCALPER is an individual who has a complete knowledge of the marketplace at his disposal. He knows who is buying, how many they are buying, and at what price they will buy; he knows who is selling, how many they are selling, and at what price they will sell. This trader is a well-known individual in the pit he inhabits because he simultaneously bids and offers contracts at every price possible. When this trader participates in trading, he is so well versed in his knowledge of the inner workings of the pit that he knows where to exit his trade even before he enters it (often called "making your second trade, first"). This ability allows him to avert losses by scratching the majority of his trades. An overwhelming influence in the marketplace, the edge trader expects to get the edge and invariably is always given it. Because he is so dominant in his trading, trading constantly all day long, his dynamic is not just scalping, but the force he brings to bear on the remainder of the trading pit. This omnipresence allows him to trade effectively due to the fact the floor brokers not only know he will

participate at any price, but they depend on him to do so, in order to fill their orders.

2. TRANSITION SCALPER - This trader primarily uses the basics of scalping with an emphasis on joining the bid and offering on the offer, but with a slight twist. The TRANSITION SCALPER is an experienced trader who purposely keeps a keen vigil on the amount of contracts that are bid and are offered. If the TRANSITION SCALPER sees that the offer is being bought or the bid is being sold, he will initiate a trade, buying the offer or selling the bid, contrary to the rule concerning getting the edge. However, by doing so, he has situated himself in a position ready for his perceived change in the market. If he is correct, when the offer becomes the new bid, or the old bid becomes the new offer, he has already situated himself to benefit from that change.

3. MOMENTUM SCALPER - The MOMENTUM SCALPER is usually an experienced trader who has developed the ability to watch the proceedings and either buy into an upwardly moving market or sell into a downwardly moving market, each time knowing just when to continue his present course. Finally, a MOMENTUM SCALPER will decide that the momentum of the market has subsided in a particular direction. When he feels that a market is over-bought or oversold, the MOMENTUM SCALPER will sell out the exact number of contracts he has been buying, or buy back the exact number of contracts he has been selling. From a flat (neither long nor short) position, the MOMENTUM SCALPER steps back, awaiting the opportunity to get in tune with the momentum of the market once again.

4. CONTRARIAN SCALPER - Working exactly like a momentum scalper, the contrarian will trade in opposition of the market's momentum, selling into an upwardly moving market and buying into a downwardly moving one. The theory here is that all markets usually move past a point of saturation of buying and selling and must eventually correct this factor. The CONTRARIAN SCALPER tries to take advantage of any pull back or upward correction by picking points to sell after a rising market or picking points to buy after a falling one.

5. INTUITIVE SCALPER - By far the most difficult to describe, the INTUITIVE SCALPER is a trader who has, usually through years of experience, an ability to know when to buy the offer or sell into the bid. Unlike the TRANSITION SCALPER who depends upon his ability to keep track of the amount of contracts bid or offered, the INTUITIVE SCALPER has developed a sixth sense that tells him when to enter and exit the market. When this feeling arises, the INTUITIVE SCALPER follows the dictates of his sixth sense. No matter what everyone else in the marketplace is doing, the INTUITIVE SCALPER does only what his inner being dictates. Unlike the other types of scalpers, the INTUITIVE SCALPER is unique in his approach to the market, for it is based solely upon his internal assessment of any and all outside stimuli.

THE POSITION TRADER

In his basic form, a POSITION TRADER buys or sells contracts and holds the position until he determines that it is time to liquidate his holdings. A POSITION TRADER may predetermine a specific profit or loss parameter with a general idea of the specific length of time, *i.e.* day, week, month, etc., it will take to determine when liquidation will take place. Unlike the scalper, in and out of the market all day long, ending the day neither long or short contracts, a POSITION TRADER anticipates having to hold on to his trade for more than one trading session or until the market reaches his predetermined point.

In any event, a POSITION TRADER is an individual who has predetermined what side of the market he wishes to place his confidence. His ability to forecast market movement is dependent upon his research of fundamental and/or technical market factors. No matter how he arrives at his specific conclusions, when a POSITION TRADER buys contracts, he is confident that the market price will rise; conversely, if he sells contracts, he is confident of declining prices. It is his willingness to have exposure to loss over an extended period of time that really differentiates him from most traders, who are generally short term in their approach to risk taking.

THE SPREADER

Another popular trading style is known as SPREADING. A SPREADER is a trader who simultaneously buys one contract and sells another. This simultaneous buying and selling may be done within the same underlying commodity (using two different delivery months— *i.e.* buy September, sell December) or between two different commodities that may or may not have a connection (*i.e.,* buy Gold sell Silver). In actuality, there are many different types of spreading techniques. It is, however, to our advantage, at this point in our discussion, that we keep our explanation at a basic level.

When a SPREADER buys one contract and sells another at the same time, he is looking for a number of possible results:

1. The SPREADER expects that the contract purchased will again in price at a faster rate than the contract sold.

INITIATE POSITION:	buy X at 7	sell Y at 5
LIQUIDATE POSITION:	sell X at 15	buy Y at 10
	Profit of 8	Loss of 5

    = Total Profit 3.

2. The SPREADER expects that the contract sold will lose value (which gains a profit for the seller) faster than the contract pur chased loses value (which incurs a loss for the buyer).

INITIATE POSITION:	buy X at 7	sell Y at 5
LIQUIDATE POSITION:	sell X at 5	buy Y at 2
	Loss of 2	Profit of 3

    = Total Profit 1.

3. The SPREADER expects that the contract bought will increase in value (a gain in profit for the buyer) and the contract sold will decrease in value (which is a gain in profit for a seller).

INITIATE POSITION:	buy X at 7	sell Y at 5
LIQUIDATION POSITION:	sell X at 15	buy Y at 3
	Profit of 8	Profit of 2

    = Total Profit of 10.

As we mentioned earlier in this chapter, there are a number of different spreading strategies that cross over the boundaries of the underlying commodities utilized by the SPREADER. Whatever the type of spread attempted, the end result desired for the SPREADER is that he is attempting to buy and sell a contract that will ultimately make a profit when the spread is exited.

SPREADING limits risk to some extent. Through the simultaneous buying and selling involved, you have both a long and short position. This type of trading is attractive because you have somewhat protected yourself from loss, if the market moves in an unfavorable direction. This method of trading is very adaptable, since it allows for versatility. A SPREADER can be a short-term trader; putting on spreads and taking them off a short time later (the same day, following day, etc.). A SPREADER can also be a long-term trader, keeping a spread in his trading account until he feels it is an appropriate time to liquidate it.

THE ADVANTAGE OF BEING ON THE TRADING FLOOR

By now, you should have a clear understanding of the different types of traders who populate the trading pit. You should also have a grasp of the trading techniques these traders employ. At this juncture, you might ask yourself, why is it necesssary to physically enter the pit in order to trade in one of the styles described? Well, it is true that you may employ any of the trading styles mentioned form off the trading floor, utilizing a brokerage house to represent your orders. However, there is a definite advantage to being a pit trader.

One main factor is cost. If you are not a member of an exchange, either through the purchase of a seat or its rental, you will pay substantially higher commission costs to have your business transacted. However, the most important reason to want to be in the pit, as opposed to trading a contract from off the floor, is called the pit trader's edge.

Earlier in our text, we mentioned the differential between to bid and offer of a contract. If you are physically in the trading pit, you will be directly involved with the actual movement of the contract's price, as it reacts to market supply and demand. As a pit trader, you gain the advantage of buying on the bid and selling on the offer. This advantage is not ordinarily afforded to orders entered into the marketplace by off-the-floor traders. As you stand in the trading arena, you will be able to react to its movement, by raising your price to buy and your offer to sell. In this way, you can take advantage of the immediacy your presence in the pit entitles you, by adjusting your bid-offer differential. If you were not in the pit physically, your order would be in the hands of a floor broker representing you. Any amendment to your order would take valuable time. If a change is necessary, off-the-floor traders are at a disadvantage to those who are able to make market adjustments as they occur. In short, you, as a pit trader, get the first shot at a market change. Orders represented on paper, through floor brokers are limited to a specific price and represented on paper, through floor brokers are limited to a specific price and may be unable to participate, if market movement precludes their execution.

And, what about market orders, orders that do not have a price, just a number of contracts to buy or sell? Don't they participate in a moving market? Well, yes they do, but this is where your presence in the pit brings its greatest advantage. Any order to buy or sell at the market is executed by buying from you on your offer, or selling to you on your bid, since you are the one determining th bid-offer differential. You, the pit trader, enjoy the advantage of buying at a lower price or selling at a higher price—the edge gained by those physically in the pit.

The negative aspect to the advantages afforded to those who work in the pits lies only in the fact that the pit, as noted in another chapter, under the heading *The Physical Factor* can be a physically exhausting place to work. To reiterate, it is not for the faint of heart or spirit. To gain and maintain the edge afforded in the pit, one must be willing to forgot the amenities of the coat and tie corporate world and its promise of offices furnished with oak desks, comfortable chairs and predetermined earnings.

Chapter II
21 Traits of a Successful Trader

In another chapter, we alerted you to the pitfalls confronting a trader. You also know what to expect in terms of competitive styles of trading and the traders who use them. Lastly, you discovered that being in the pit, physically, may be preferable to all other venues of trading. With all of this in mind, you continue your quest for more.

It is now time to examine the individual trader more closely. What does the successful trader look like and how does a successful trader act when engaged in the business of trading for a living? Armed with all the facts and observations we have supplied, you now want to know what it really takes to make it.

THE SUCCESSFUL PIT TRADER

In the world of trading, success is judged by your bottom line. Those who are successful, the million dollar earners, eventually obtain a reputation. Once established, this reputation for success is self-fulfilling. The reason for self-fulfillment is that all million-dollar earners exhibit certain traits that lend themselves to creating an image of profitability. Let's examine these traits and compare them with the traits exhibited by unsuccessful traders, those who have not established this aura of success. In essence, this is what a successful trader looks and acts like during his battle in the trading pit:

21 TRAITS OF A SUCCESSFUL PIT TRADER

$PT Successful Pit Trader. A Person Who Looks, Acts and Is Successful.

UPT = Unsuccessful Pit Trader. A Person Looking for Fast, Easy Money who is Unwilling to Put Forth the Effort Necessary to be Successful.

#1   STABLE IN HIS SELF-IMAGE

$PT loves to trade. He is prepared and trades instinctively. His demeanor remains constant, whether he makes a winning or losing trade.

UPT's personality changes, depending on whether he is making or losing money. His demeanor is observable and transparently different when his decisions result in losses.

#2   CONFIDENT AND SELF ASSURED

$PT confidently acts and reacts to the flow of the market. When trading, he enters and exits the market with self-assurance that would convince any observer each trade is a winning one.

UPT is unsure of when to enter and when to exit the market. He makes it painfully obvious if his decision has been an incorrect one.

#3   ASSERTIVE AND AGRESSIVE

$PT expends every bit of a seemingly unlimited source of energy to get as many trades as he can. He demonstrates, through voice and body language, that he wants and expects every trade.

UPT screams and hopes to get a trade he really does not deserve. While he has his head and eyes down, with his arms barely above his head, he puts forth a half-hearted attempt to be noticed.

#4   AWARENESS

$PT knows the market, the market movers, brokers, and traders. While continually storing and updating all information concerning orders in the pit, he keeps a close watch on brokers and traders to whom he can turn, at a moment's notice, to buy or sell contracts in a moving market.

UPT does not bother to know the floor brokers and traders moving the market. He does not know, nor bother to keep track, of who is doing what, which prevents him from gaining the edge at the appropriate moment.

#5   CALM AND RELAXED

$PT maintains an inner quietness, to prevent getting emotionally involved and caught up in the excitement of the pit. He maintains a relaxed attitude, even in the face of adversity.

UPT gets involved in the yelling and screaming and cannot decide what to do next. When he does trade, he holds onto trades, hoping that losers will become winners and winners will become bigger winners.

#6   ANTICIPATORY AND INTUITIVE

$PT, through preparation, study, and experience, has learned to anticipate market movement. Utilizing a developed sense of intuition, he executes his trades.

UPT believes he possesses "Market Feel" from day one. He lacks experience and does not have the ability to recognize market trends. He views preparation and study as a waste of time.

#7 Rested, Physically Fit and Emotionally Sound

$PT gets plenty of sleep and rest. He regularly participates in some form of exercise, which relieves stress, enabling him to trade with a clear mind. He never allows his personal problems to accompany him into the trading pit.

UPT is confident he can drink and party late into the night, even though he has to trade the following day. The pressure from trading zaps his energy and makes him too tired to exercise. He has difficulty escaping his personal problems; frequently blaming them as causes for losing trading days.

#8 Stoical and Focused

$PT remains an enigma to his fellow traders—they never know if he has made or lost money. He also has the ability to keep his attention completely centered on the key players and brokers in the marketplace.

UPT, on the other hand, shows both his euphoria and his disappointment, by demonstrating his emotions through his actions. Whether he is making or losing money can be determined by his personality, moment by moment. No matter which is the case, all of his mood swings cause him to be distracted from the business of trading.

#9 Mentally Alert, Determined and Patient

$PT has an inner calmness that allows him to be ready to deal with any challenge. He is a competitor, bound and determined to make money, willingly exerting whatever effort is necessary. Also, $PT realizes that it takes time to develop the skills to trade and the endurance to stay in the pit all day.

UPT is distracted by the constant chatter of an indecisive inner voice. Easily discouraged, he is unable to deal with failure. He expects to earn a living without a concentrated effort. Impatient, he is plagued by erratic trading behavior. UPT feels that he already possesses the skills to make money and doesn't think it is necessary to stay in the pit all day.

#10 Silent

$PT maintains a quiet demeanor throughout the day. This allows him to concentrate on the business of trading.

UPT is busy talking to whomever will talk to him, about everything from sports to sex. His inattentiveness causes him to miss trades during the course of business.

#11 Workaholic

$PT loves to trade and remains in the pit all day. He does take time off, when his positions allow or when he feels it is necessary for his mental health.

UPT looks for reasons to leave the trading pit during the day. He will even make up excuses for not remaining in the pit, such as it is not busy, it is a good day for golf, or he has made enough money for the day.

#12 Resilient

$PT makes both winning and losing trades. He determines the result of his trading at the end of each trading day. He keeps an upbeat attitude in the face of an unprofitable day. Undeterred by failure, he vows to do better tomorrow.

UPT spends useless time and energy during the trading day delighting in his winners and mourning his losers. If his losers outpace his winners, UPT becomes inordinately depressed by the outcome. In the final examination, his trading suffers from his inability to bounce back from defeat.

#13   ADAPTABLE

$PT adjusts his trading style to fit market opportunity. Since he would rather trade than do anything else for a living, he is willing to change his trading style to fit the needs of both busy and slow market conditions.

UPT has difficulty adjusting when markets change. Fixed on one methodology, he struggles to succeed in the face of market conditions that do not fit his trading style. Eventually, he may even consider another career, rather than making necessary changes to his trading.

#14   ADEPT AT STAYING IN THE PRESENT

$PT is centered in the here and now. He gives no thought to what may occur or might have occurred. Realizing that history may or may not repeat itself, $pt concentrates on the business at hand, keeping an eye on those market players with whom he can best maximize his profits.

UPT dwells on past trades. He deludes himself into thinking that, if a market strategy worked in the past, it will surely work again (although nothing could be further from the truth). UPT fantasizes about all the big trades he will make in the future, and his day-dreaming constantly distracts him from what he should be presently concentrating.

#15   OPEN-MINDED

$PT has no opinion regarding the direction of the market. He remains ready and willing to trade whatever opportunity is afforded him.

UPT knows it all. He believes he can predict market direction and refuses to become a believer when the market plainly shows him something other than what he anticipated. The market punishes him for his inflexibility.

#16 Reflective

$PT At the end of the day, examines his trading behavior. He reviews the good and the bad, resolving not to repeat his errors.

UPT is just glad the day is over. He decides that preparation for tomorrow is a waste of time, and anyways, his errors today were not really his fault, just bad luck.

#17 Remarkable Memory

$PT has a deliberate memory, storing trading information from days, weeks, and even months in the past. He has the ability to recall this information, using it to his advantage.

UPT does not pay attention. He can not tell you where the market has traded, nor can he identify if market movers have bought or sold contracts. Therefore, he cannot really use the information he has been given to his advantage.

#18 Courageous

$PT is a player and can trade any market, at any time. He is aware of his own capabilities and stays within his own limits. If his preparation and research tells him to, he will fearlessly buy, when others are selling and vice versa.

UPT cannot bring himself to trade when the market moves unexpectedly, fearing that he may lose money. He is constantly looking for the right spot to get in the market, but somehow cannot get himself to *"pull the trigger."* Often, he wishes he had acted, long after opportunity has passed him by.

#19 Insightful of his Self-Destructive Tendency

$PT knows himself and recognizes his inner tendency to be self-destructive. If he begins to feel the need to recoup losses by risking more money than usual, $PT will remove himself from the pit to settle down, get back to square one, and return to his normal trading groove.

UPT does not recognize nor understand his self-destructive behavior. When he begins trading poorly, UPT panics and over-trades. By increasing the number of contracts traded, he risks more money to recoup his losses. By the end of the day, his inability to identify this self-destructive behavior has left him without hope, or money.

#20 Honest and Fair

$PT is honest and fair. When trading, he is mindful of the rules and abides by them. He reports his trades to exchange personnel for price dissemination as soon as possible. He immediately checks his trades with opposing brokers and traders to reconcile price and quantity. When a miscommunication occurs, he does his best to settle the dispute in a just and truthful manner, even if it results in a trading loss.

UPT wants everyone and everything to follow his agenda. He is obsessed with making money and will even circumvent the rules in order to reach his goal. His actions, when dealing with others, expose his greedy, unscrupulous nature. By not following the procedures expected of him, he has more mismatched trades than most traders. When dealing with his miscommunications, he unwillingly refuses to compromise with others, even if he is the party at fault.

#21 Reasonable in his Expectations

$PT believes in doing the best he can, while never allowing himself to stray too far from his goal of being a profitable trader. His strategy is to make a number of small profits on a large number of trades. In this way, $PT builds profits through consistent trading behavior.

UPT has no set routine and is erratic in his daily trading. His strategy is to wait for the optimum opportunity and "hit the home run" on one or two trades each trading session. He wants too much, too fast, and is unwilling to keep his expectations at the reasonable level necessary to be successful in the trading game.

As you can well determine by this profile of our $uccessful and Unsuccessful Pit Traders, the composite makeup of a trader who succeeds at the trading game is a complicated mix of many qualities – some inherent, some learned. Examine the profile carefully, being especially honest with yourself in your estimation of your ability to be more like $PT than UPT. No one is exactly like either of the two traders portrayed in this chapter. However, all of the positive qualities mentioned are desirable and will make success much more attainable, if some measure of each is included in the trading arsenal of aspiring traders.

Chapter III
What Does It Take to be a Successful Trader?

"Winning isn't everything, it is the only thing," is a quotation attributed to the legendary Green Bay Packer Coach, Vince Lombardi. The sentiment expressed by this adage seems to exemplify the underlying credo of the pit trader: the purpose of playing is winning, the purpose of trading is making money. However, there is much more involved in trading than just a burgeoning bottom line, for winning and making money are just the end result of the total process.

Having progressed this far in your education, you are just about ready to venture into the trading arena. You understand markets, market movement, and market players. You possess intimate knowledge of the pits organization, and function. Unfortunately, all of this knowledge will be of no value if your reason for learning is not based on an inner drive to compete and succeed at your chosen endeavor. In the beginning of our journey, we questioned your motivation for choosing trading as a career. You have come a long way since those questions were asked of you. If, however, after all that you now know, your answer is that you are motivated solely by money, then the odds are highly stacked against your success.

YOU GOTTA LUV IT!

The mystery is solved, the game of twenty questions is over. The real secret is out. All along you thought that a valid reason for becoming a trader was to make money, *"...winning is the only thing!"* as the Coach said. If, however, you could question the most successful traders in the business and force them to tell you one truth and nothing but one truth, you would probably be astounded by your discovery. Successful traders simply **LOVE TO TRADE!**

To these million dollar earners, money is a bonus, an extra nicety. The real focus of their trading motivation is the challenge, the competition, winning! Not to totally underplay the role of money in the equation of trading, of course, it is a necessity. You, the new trader, must be motivated by the inner need to succeed, to play the game to the best of your ability, and to beat the odds stacked against you.

Trading is stress. Trading is pressure. The stress is derived from the physical nature of the business. The pressure emanates from the need to make the right decisions, time after time, day after day, in a never-ending succession. You are only as good as your last trade. You have to prove yourself each time you set foot into the arena. All of these factors put pressure on the individual to succeed. So, you must stand in the pit and endure the physical and mental stress and pressure of this business. You have to **LOVE** what you are doing, or you will never have the desire or the endurance to continue.

A POSITIVE MENTAL ATTITUDE

Without a doubt, trading's single most important psychological factor deals with the individuals frame of mind. The first and foremost necessity to be a successful trader is a positive mental attitude. Since trading is decision making, you must be confident in yourself and your ability to make decisions. Without confidence and a positive attitude, second-guessing yourself may cause you to hesitate or even hold back completely, when opportunities arise. Hesitation is deadly to someone who makes his living by being first to respond to a bid or offer.

LIVE TO TRADE

A successful trader is an individual who cannot wait to get into the pit each day. He lives and breathes trading. He wants to participate in each and every trade. All aspects of the market fascinate him and he eagerly educates himself to further his understanding of his chosen profession.

Finally, if you live to trade, you will be motivated to improve and expand your trading horizons.

THE ABILITY TO MAINTAIN CONCENTRATION

Although trading may look like a jumbled mess to the uninitiated, in reality, it is a ballet of movement and sound designed to afford liquidity to the public and ensure the safe transference of risk from one party to another. When one is involved with the business of trading, it is important that the intrinsically physical aspect does not distract you. You must be able to focus on your task as a trader, unwavering in your concentration. Using all of your senses, you must zero in on your task as ferociously as possible. This ability to stay focused is paramount, if you are to succeed, especially when the frenzy around you can easily engulf and sweep you away from your intended plan. Always keep your focus on your goal and you must not be distracted by anyone or anything around you. If you can steady yourself in the midst of the everyday distractions of trading, you will be, in the long run, A WINNER..

REALISTIC EXPECTATIONS

Each day, just as you prepare yourself with the technical tools at your disposal to help you make your trading decisions, you must also examine your expectations, to ensure that you are firmly grounded in reality. After some initial experience, a trader begins to know his limitations and should redefine his expectations accordingly. If you realize that you can comfortably make a given number of dollars each day without exceeding the limitations of your game plan, then, in that regard, you should not enter the pit with unrealistic expectations. Sure, on a good day you should endeavor to make as much as you can, but not in a way that will jeopardize your ability to come back and trade again the next day. Each day you should follow your game plan and aim to earn a predetermined realistic amount. We believe that you should continue to stretch the envelope and grow, but we do caution you to accompany your growth with patience, and reasonable expectations.

Loving to trade and living to trade will enable you to sustain your enthusiasm for the task at hand.

SECTION V
So You Want to Be a Trader

Chapter I
Three Important Decisions

DECISIONS, DECISIONS, DECISIONS

Trading is about decision-making and responding to the outcomes of your decisions. In an in-depth examination of the process of trading, you would come to realize that trading consists of one decision after another in an endless continuum. As we mentioned earlier in our text, each individual trade is a microcosm of one evaluation after another of whether to buy or sell, how many contracts should be involved, which way the market will move next, etc. If you are at all hesitant when it is time to take a stand, you will not be an effective trader.

However, for the aspiring trader, trading represents more than just the decisions one faces in the context of an ordinary trading day. The newcomer faces a multitude of decisions even before his first trade is executed. In this chapter, we will examine a few of the important matters that must be considered before entering into one's first trade.

WHICH PIT DO I TRADE?

Assuming you are ready to step into the pit to begin trading, you must first decide where you will trade. No one starts the car and begins driving before deciding where the final destination will be. Likewise, in trading, one should choose a place to trade before beginning to trade, but there is a lot more here to be considered than meets the eye.

Each individual trading pit has its own personality. The uniqueness of each pit is determined by a number of different factors, but by and large, no matter the influence of factors, no two trading pits are alike. Some pits are small with few traders standing in them, while others are enormous, filled with hundreds of traders. It is hard to determine which came first, the number of traders due directly to the size of the pit, or the size of the pit due to the number of traders who call it home. Whatever the reason, some trading pits are small because the volume of contracts traded each day is not large enough to support a larger population of participants.

Although a pit may be small in physical size and number of traders, neither is reason to disregard it as a possible trading venue. It is true that small pits may have lower trading volume, but this does not mean that one cannot make a living trading in one of these places. Unfortunately, the hierarchy of the smaller pit is tightly woven. It is much harder to gain acceptance in a smaller pit, since the existing traders do not wish to alter their trading relationships or further divide the already small volume of contracts traded. However, with enough perseverance, a new trader may be able to ensconce himself into a trading niche in one of the smaller pits; if he is willing to endure the inevitable period of rejection from veteran traders.

In opposition, you will find a considerable difference in the ambience of the enormous trading pits, such as the **Chicago Mercantile Exchange's Standard & Poor 500** pit or the **Chicago Board of Trade's U.S. Treasury Bond** pit. These massive bodies of humanity are among the largest in the world, and they are perfect examples of all of the idiosyncrasies of pit trading. Each contains the usual pit hierarchy, consisting of top step floor brokers surrounded by local traders willing to trade large numbers of contracts, followed by the other brokers and traders of smaller volume as described earlier in our text. Each of these pits has a high volume of contracts traded each day, allowing the trader a measure of easy execution in buying and selling with the edge desired to make money. However, along with the advantage of liquidity comes the dog-eat-dog competition one would expect in such a marketplace. It is wise to remember that the larger the volume of contracts traded each day in a particular pit, the better the chances for an individual trader to make a living. So one must weigh the difference in competitive attitude that may vary from a low volume pit in relation to a high volume one.

As can be expected, there are many pits of various sizes. Again, each pit has its own personality, whether it is somewhat intimate characteristic of a smaller trading pit, or impersonal and highly competitive characteristic of the behemoths mentioned as examples. It is for you, the aspiring trader, to find the place in which you feel most comfortable and confident to begin your trading career.

WHERE DO I STAND?

Once you have determined which trading pit you will spend the majority of your trading day, you must next decide where in the pit is the most advantageous place for you to stand. Part of this decision will be made for you, since, as we explained in a previous chapter, all pits have a hierarchy determined by the amount of contracts you are willing to trade at any given time.

To reiterate briefly, in almost every trading pit, floor brokers populate the top step of the pit where they can easily receive incoming orders. Brokers who buy and sell large quantities of contracts in single trades are the usual occupants of the top step, since they have the most orders coming into the pit. These top step brokers want to have local traders around them who will facilitate the execution of these large orders by buying or selling almost any given amount these brokers announce. Also, the fewer traders a broker interacts with, the lesser the chance for miscommunication and error. Therefore, the top step of the pit is almost always reserved for brokers surrounded by traders, one step below, who have established themselves as being willing to assure the risk of trading a large volume of contracts. Since new traders are not encouraged to begin their careers by jumping into the game by assuming a huge amount of risk this type of trading incurs, new traders need not incorporate this place in the pit as a possible starting point.

Given the normal course of events, new traders are usually relegated to the least desirable spots in the pit, away from floor brokers. The flat surface of the pit below the bottom step is populated by the new arrivals hoping to work their way up, step by step, to a more desirable place in the pit. The decision of where to stand is usually determined for you. Once you have established yourself as a trader, then the process of moving up the steps begins.

Just because you are exiled to the least desirable level of the pit does not mean that you should not endeavor to maneuver yourself as close to a floor broker as you possibly can. Sometimes, during the course of a trading day, spots open up when other traders leave the pit. If this opportunity arises, you should always take it, and move as close to a floor broker as you possibly can. In doing so, the broker will become familiar with your voice, presence, and acronym. (a designation given to you by the exchange and worn on your trading jacket to identify you as a participant in a trade). This familiarity will enhance your chances in executing a trade with the broker, hopefully giving you the trading edge to buy on the bid or to sell on the offer.

When examined closely, it is apparent that placement in the pit is a great importance. Since most traders in a pit will most likely force you into starting at the bottom, making the best of your position may make the difference in success or failure during the infancy of your trading career.

WITH WHOM DO I TRADE?

As we have pointed out a number of times, your job as an individual trader is to make a market: to buy a contract on the bid and sell it on the offer —this important relationship is known as getting the edge. All traders WANT TO GAIN THE EDGE, a distinct advantage of being on the trading floor, physically in the trading pit. Trading with brokers to gain the edge is the primary focus of the individual pit trader.

Let's set up a typical scenario of trading in the pit on a day to day basis. You enter your chosen pit and stand in your usual spot as close to a floor broker as possible. When trading commences, you begin repeating the price at which you wish to purchase contracts and a price that you wish to sell them. For example, you make a two sided market by yelling, "30 bid for one, sell one at 40!" Which means that you are willing to pay 30 to buy a contract and sell one contract at 40. A broker, recognizing your voice and determining that you are the first trader he has heard "bidding 30" to buy one contract, motions to you that he will sell you one contract at a price of 30. You have now established that you have gained the edge on one contract, buying it at the lower price of 30, your bid price. Looking and listening, you determine that other traders in the pit are also seeking to buy contracts at 30 and sell them at 40.

You hear a broker, who is bidding to buy a contract by yelling, "30 for one," and you respond by yelling, "One at 40!" Luckily, he sees you, hears your voice first, and gestures that he will buy one contract from you at a price of 40. You have just made your first complete trade of the day and it is a profitable one. You continue along in the same manner, attempting to buy contracts at 30 and sell them at 40. You have completed a number of successful trades, when you sense a change in the market, initiated by increased activity and accompanied by the fact that you are unable to hear as many voices offering to sell contracts at the 40 level. In fact, a broker announces to the pit that he is willing to buy all of the contracts at 40, at which time he buys the few remaining contracts offered at 40. The broker then continues bidding 40 for the additional contracts necessary to complete his order.

The market has just moved from "30 bid at 40", to "40 bid at 50". You, also, begin to change your bid and offer prices in order to compete for the edge by buying on the new bid of 40 and selling on the new offer of 50. With the new market prices established, you are able to buy a contract at 40 and sell a contract at 50 on a couple of occasions. However, you buy another contract at 40, but you are unsuccessful in selling one at 50. Through a repeated number of attempts, you try to sell it at the higher price but cannot. As you listen to the buying and selling taking place around you, you notice that fewer and fewer voices are expressing a willingness to purchase a contract at 40. Deciding that the market may again change in price, this time shifting downward instead of upward, you decide to sell the contract for which you have paid 40, to the next broker or trader who voices a 40 bid. It so happens, that a local trader near you, who is not a floor broker, yells, "40 bid at 50!" You immediately respond by yelling, "Sell you 1 at 40," as you motion, with your palm facing away from your body, your willingness to sell one contract at 40. The opposing trader acknowledges his acceptance and writes your acronym on his trading card with the appropriate information, and you do the same. After a few seconds elapse, allowing the other trader to finish writing, you immediately check with the trader to confirm that you did sell him one contract at 40. He acknowledges this fact verbally. The act of verification a short time after making a trade is called "checking a trade," and it is extremely important to do so, as soon as you are able, in order to prevent errors from occurring.

In the transaction you have checked, two things have occurred. First, you have made a trade where you purchased a contract and sold a contract at the same price, a trade known as a "scratch"; also, you have broken an unwritten rule of trading by trading with someone who is not a floor broker. However, you feel you are justified in giving up your edge to another local trader, because you felt it was the best way from preventing a trading loss. In this case, you rationalized that it was best to sacrifice your edge in anticipation of market movement. In a matter of moments, your anticipation proves to be true, when the market reverts back to a "30 bid at 40" market quote.

It is obvious that trading is all about questions and the decisions resulting from answering those questions. Your concerns as a new trader will first be focused on: which pit is the right pit for your trading style, where should you stand in that pit, and with whom should you endeavor to trade.

Before you make your first decision resulting in your first trade, you will have faced a myriad of possibilities and, we hope, chosen wisely.

NOTE: It is best to trade with a broker as often as possible, since he is the one person who may want to trade with you again and again—giving you, the trader, the edge.

NOTE: The market movement used in this chapter moves at ten point increments, *i.e.* 00 to 10, 10 to 20, & 20 to 30, etc., similar to the movement of the **S&P 500 Futures** at the **Chicago Mercantile Exchange.**

Chapter II
Five Trading Problems That You Cannot Anticipate

EXTERNAL SOURCES OF PROBLEMS

To some extent, in most human endeavors, those who are on the inside want those on the outside kept out. If exclusion is not possible, then those who are in power want those who attempt to join them to pay a price for acceptance into "the in-crowd" or "the club." You may have seen it in many forms throughout your life's experiences: upperclassmen harassing underclassmen, fraternity members hazing pledges, or veteran members initiating rookies. All of these rituals are designed to make it difficult, if not impossible, for the newcomer to earn the rite of membership. It is no different in the trading pit. When established, traders are faced with accepting a newcomer, a message is sent: all newcomers must "pay their dues" to earn acceptance. The behavior of the veteran traders conveying this message is **less** than subtle.

However, since you have made the effort to learn, we feel that you have earned the right to this closely guarded information. Through our insider's knowledge, we will prepare you for the realities awaiting you, as you begin your career. Usually, these secrets are closely guarded and not discussed outside of the trading fraternity. We feel that you have "paid your dues," so here are a few more insights into the world of commodity pit trading.

#1 IT'S NOT THAT WE DON'T LIKE YOU, BUT JUST GO AWAY

When you first enter a pit and it becomes apparent to the established members that you may be considering their trading domain as a possible home, you may encounter a unique type of "defending-my-turf" behavior.

Pit behavior is not conducted by corporate social rules; no one is bound by formality to be superficially social, much less civil, in the trading arena. This is the ultimate, individualistic entrepreneurial endeavor. Unlike an employee starting a new job with a company, personal greetings and well wishes are nonexistent. While others may share conversation or a joke during slack times, the new trader is usually ignored. It will soon become painfully obvious that you have attempted to enter a closed society.

Even if you were to attempt to converse with another trader, discuss market dynamics, or seek advice, for the most part, little will be revealed to you. If you want to be included in a trade, when the number of contracts are split up among a group of traders, be prepared to be overlooked. Remember that you are the uninvited. Brokers are unaccustomed to your presence, so they will even unintentionally overlook you.

At this point, you may be asking yourself, how and when does a new trader get to be a regular member of the group? If you:

1. stick to your resolve
2. show up each day, ready to trade while remaining aggressive, almost to a fault, and
3. display the perseverance necessary to overcome all obstacles placed before you

Eventually the other members will realize that you are not going to go away. When this realization hits them, your acceptance will begin. This, by no means, entitles you to full benefits as a pit member. Those are earned through hard work and participation in the day to day process of trading.

#2 BIDING YOUR TIME WHILE LOOKING FOR AN OPENING

Since you will be stuck in no man's land down in the bottom of the pit at the beginning of the day, you may begin to feel some resentment at being so far from the action. Take heart! There may be a silver lining in this dark cloud.

A new trader faces the most risk of error at two crucial times of the day: just after the opening bell and just before the closing bell to end trading. During these two highly frenetic times of the trading day, prices usually fluctuate wildly. It is at this time that the pit experiences its greatest population density. All of the traders native to that trading arena usually make it a practice to be in the pit for the opening and the closing. Since prices jump around the most at these times, the veteran traders view these peak minutes as the optimum for making the most money. What does this have to do with you, the new trader? The answer lies in the time between the first and last hour and a half of the day.

After the initial swings of the day, many markets settle down into reasonable trading ranges, unless there are mitigating factors causing unrest in the marketplace. When involatile markets drift up and down, sometimes pits begin to empty, due to trader boredom or the perception that not much will happen until that closing hour and a half. When this attrition occurs, the new trader should seize the opportunity. During these sparsely populated segments of the day, the new trader should do his best to move into the spaces vacated by the absent traders, to get as close to the floor brokers as possible. Also, when markets have small ranges, the risk involved is less. This scenario lends itself perfectly to the new trader, who is now ensconced in a more advantageous trading spot while the lack of competition and the small range of prices afford him the opportunity to practice his chosen profession.

Although you already know that you must end the day back in "no man's land", by biding your time during the middle of the day, a new trader can take advantage of the opportunity afforded him when it presents itself. Remember that patience is truly a virtue in this situation.

#3 YOU CAN STAND IN THE PIT, BUT YOU CAN'T PLAY

As if it isn't enough that you will be ignored and ostracized when you first enter the pit, there are even more devious tricks awaiting you when you begin your trading. As we mentioned, your fellow traders want you to leave. If you are insensitive enough to endure their social wall of indifference, there are other ways for them to get their message across.

One type of trick that you should be aware of is the **SHUTOUT**. In a shutout, other traders will gobble up all of the contracts available for purchase or sale, eliminating the possibility of a broker splitting up the contracts among a number of traders. If you can't get a piece of a trade, maybe you'll go away!

Another simple way of undermining a new trader is the **BLOCKOUT**. A blockout is when other traders physically try to block another trader's view of the broker who is bidding or offering contracts. If others can block you from view, it will decrease the likelihood that the broker may both see and hear your response. If a broker cannot see or hear you, effectively, you do not exist.

And if having a conspiracy working against you to make you give up and quit is not enough, as a new trader, you are also at a disadvantage in general. As an example of this disadvantage, let's examine a typical situation that occurs many times during the course of a normal day. A broker announces an order. On occasion, a broker may not be certain which trader was the first to respond. If the broker picks the wrong respondent, an established veteran, who feels that he has been overlooked, will forthrightly tell the broker of this perceived injustice. However, if a newcomer should be the rightful participant inadvertently omitted from the trade, his accusation of incompetence on the broker's part would be looked upon as a direct insult. The new trader would be branded as a trouble-maker, someone who is trying to make the broker look foolish. Be careful if this should occur. In the case of a veteran, another established trader may come to his support; as a new trader, no one will corroborate your contention, an omission intended to undermine your status as an accepted member of the pit. Again, the establishment will work, ever so subtly, to make you want to go elsewhere to work.

In any number of ingenious ways, established traders may respond to a new trader's presence by subtly sabotaging his ability to participate in the trading process, all the while, staying within the rules of the exchange. At this point, you may be asking yourself, why do these traders go to such extremes to eliminate the newcomer? In many cases, other traders see the appearance of a new local as a threat to their livelihood and survival. The behavior they exhibit, both professionally and socially, toward a novice pit member is a reaction to the possibility that the intruder, as they see you, may in some way interfere with their ability to continue to be successful.

Finally, in response to all of the tricks leveled against you, we can only counsel you to stick with your plans. As we have advised you throughout our text, perseverance is the only defensive measure that will counteract these attempts to make you disappear. So, your strength of purpose is your true ally in this regard.

#4 IMMEDIATE GRATIFICATION —BEWARE!

In a world filled with a sense of urgency: cash on demand from an ATM, cellular phones for instant communication, on-line information available 24 hours a day on the internet, drive-thru fast food, etc., an individual may find that a need for instant gratification has crept into one's subconscious. No longer are we patient, when it comes to the things we want in life. Is it any wonder, that this may also become a problem for a new trader, when it comes to preparing oneself to succeed?

Although we have dispelled the myths about the stereotypical commodity trader, some of the notions concerning instant success and big money may persist. If these ill-conceived ideas remain in any form, they will most certainly sabotage a new trader. Even though we have repeated this concept over and over in our text, some potential traders may still balk at the acceptance of the idea that trading commodities is just plain, hard work. Coupled with this misconception of easy money, anyone laboring with the need for immediate gratification is destined for failure.

Do not enter the trading arena with any expectation of instant success. Pay your dues, take your time, eliminate your weaknesses, and experience the process of trading. Trading is an evolving entity that is not easily mastered. Realistically, even under the best of circumstances, a new trader should only expect to break even in his first year.

#5 THE PRINCIPLE OF SELF-DESTRUCTION

The principle of self-destruction is based upon a new trader's inability to accept a loss. A veteran trader shrugs off losses and the process of trading goes on. To an experienced trader, losers, as well as winners, are equally accepted as part of the business. The result of his trading does not affect his trading behavior nor his psychological frame of mind.

For a new trader, accepting a loss is more difficult, if not impossible. When a new trader fails to exit a trade that continues to move against him, a number of things begin to happen. By failing to react, whether or not he has the opportunity to do so, he begins to feel a sense of terror from the ever increasing loss and a dread that he will not be able to stop it from getting worse. As the loss continues to mount, his stomach clenches into a leaden knot, his blood pressure skyrockets, and his reasoning deserts him. When he finally summons the resolve to eliminate the enormous burden this losing trade has placed upon his shoulders, another whole set of emotions awaits him.

Emotional exhaustion, stemming from the entire scenario, over-takes the trader. Sweating, limp, and depressed, a new trader will begin the next step toward self-destruction by calculating exactly to the penny, the amount of his loss. When this realization hits, the real trouble begins. First, there comes an overwhelming sense of helplessness. In this context, helplessness results from a feeling that an impossible task looms ahead. A new trader, used to making progress in small, incremental steps, believes he is now faced with the job of making back a great deal of money in a very short time.

Helplessness is followed by desperation. Faced with less money in his account, a new trader rapidly reviews his financial responsibili-ties and the ever-increasing possibility that he will not be able to meet them. Unhappy with the turn of events, and saddled with a strong sense of guilt because he did not follow his adopted set of trading rules, he becomes desperate to alter the outcome of his ac-tions. Irrationally, he decides that the only way to achieve his goal to make back the money he just lost is to increase the number of contracts he trades. His plan is to increase his risk from one con-tract per trade to five contracts per trade.

In this fragile state of mind, a new trader cannot handle any more adversity. Unfortunately, his new plan does not exclude further losses. Sure, if he is correct, he makes more money per trade; if he is wrong, however, he loses more. At this point, additional losses will occur and self-destruction will continue. If he does not remove himself from the trading pit, the result may even be career ending.

How does one stay clear of this self-destructive mode?

1.   The most obvious answer is to remain calm and disciplined under all circumstances.

2.   You must stay within the confines of the rules you have established for trading, specifically the one that deals with taking losses as soon as possible.

3.   You must learn to be aware that you are exhibiting the initial signs of self-destructive behavior. If you experience a loss, and it becomes a focal point in your trading behavior, stop trading. Step away from the situation, physically leave the pit if you must, but remove yourself from the temptation of remaining and making any decisions in that frame of mind.

4.   Look to the veteran trader as your model. He accepts losses unemotionally, with optimum recovery time. Strive to emulate his example, so that you too, can suffer a loss, no matter how great, recover, focus, and continue without missing a beat of the market's rhythm.

Chapter III
The Six Secrets of Trading

No matter how prepared an individual is, when a new trader steps into the pit for the first time, he is usually overwhelmed by the noise and movement all around him. The initial impression the novice has, when entering the pit for the first time, is that the veteran traders are extremely aggressive. They ferociously attack incoming orders like hungry lions feasting on prey. In the eyes of the neophyte, these veterans' hunger to grab a piece of each and every trade, as though their very life depends on it.

Observing this aggressive behavior first hand, most new traders seem to arrive at the same conclusion about what they are witnessing; *what do they know that I do not? Why do they forge ahead so confidently, all the while appearing as if they are positive that their actions are following the correct course?* In essence, most new traders look around the pit and arrive at the same misconception—the other traders must know more than I do.

This all too common misconception must be addressed immediately and debunked. The real truth is that all players step into the arena of trading without the benefit of precognition —nobody knows for certain what will happen. Unless you possess some supernatural powers to predict the future, you will enter the trading pit each day with the same opportunities as your trading competitors. With that incorrect observation aside, this chapter will take a look at other possible trouble spots for a new trader that may not be as obvious as others, but nevertheless, may cause you to stumble and fall on your road to success.

SECRET #1
YOU ARE NOT YOUR TRADE

The very first rule to establish for yourself when you begin trading is one that concerns itself with separation. Before you trade one contract, make sure that you understand that trading is a separate entity from you. Trading is a profession, a business, a livelihood, but it is not you. Give it your utmost without reserve, do the best you are capable of doing, but never judge your personal sense of worth in relation to your trading. This may seem like unnecessary advice, but personal experience and observation on our part has led us to believe that many traders begin to equate themselves with the success or failure of their trades.

If we go back a step, it will become clear how this can happen. As we stated in the beginning of this chapter, no one can predict the future; therefore, everyone is on even ground when they step into the pit to make everyday decisions concerning buying and selling contracts. Since this is the case, it is inevitable that each and every trader will have off days, no matter how well they prepare themselves for the myriad of possibilities each day can bring. If having losing trades, a losing day, a losing week, and even a losing month are possible, you must prepare yourself for that possibility.

A problem arises when a trader starts to get down on himself for losing money. As long as you can honestly say to yourself that you have done everything you can to prepare yourself to trade, and that you have followed all of your rules of discipline regarding trading, then you must accept losing as part of the trading process. Unfortunately, not all traders can reconcile themselves to this fact of life and they begin to think and act negatively.

Although you may say to yourself that this could never happen to you, this type of thinking, at times, is difficult to avoid. The constant possibility of losses from trading always hangs overhead. If you are on a losing streak, it is not too difficult to fall into this negative thinking pattern. Again, the one thing you must remember is that your worth as a person is much different than your personal financial worth.

SECRET #2
ACCEPTING A LOSS EVERYDAY

The seasoned trader knows that some trades work well, others do not. As a trader, you may make a decision that is correct for the moment. However, something unforeseen or totally unanticipated may take place, causing your once solid decision to disintegrate in a nanosecond, even before you finish writing the trade on your trading card. This type of experience is not only common, experienced traders expect it. Unfortunately, new traders often hope that each and every trade will bring success. If you spend the majority of each and every trading day hoping, then you will be out of the business before you realize it. As we mentioned in the previous discussion, the inevitability of loss in trading is as much an integral part of the process as winning. It is how you deal with the two that is important.

Do not spend your time passively in the pit; emulate the aggressiveness of the veterans. Get into the mix and trade! If you make a trade and it does not turn out as you anticipated, accept the loss, take the loss as quickly as possible by exiting the trade, put the entire trade behind you, and then take advantage of the next opportunity. That is what is happening when you observe the other traders around you – their aggressiveness is really an attempt to take advantage of opportunity, in this case, the order flow coming into the pit. You must understand that losing is a part of trading. Learn to accept it as such, never let it affect you as a person, and discipline yourself to process a trading loss as quickly as possible, so that you do not dwell on it and miss the opportunity to make your next trade a winning one.

SECRET #3
DON'T LET A WINNER TURN INTO A LOSER

One of the most baffling aspects of trading to a newcomer is the actual decision making process. Whether it is the decision to buy or sell, the act of making a decision can often take on mystical proportions to the beginning trader. The neophyte must learn quickly that trading is a commitment—either short term or long term, for the assumption of risk brought on by buying or selling a contract. It is that first hurdle, making a trade, that usually is the most difficult to maneuver.

Once a new trader realizes that no trader is absolutely positive the trade he is making is a winning one, the faster the new trader will be able to get into the process of trading. The myth that the seemingly confident trader knows something more than anyone else is just that—myth! Once a beginning trader understands that **an integral part of trading is just getting into the game and trading,** the faster the trader will come to realize that trading consists of winners and losers. The real secret is to have more winners than losers.

The next aspect of discovery regarding the decision-making process of trading deals with discipline and how it is carried out. We have also stated, again and again, that these rules are established through hard work and preparation that gets the trader ready to make intelligent decisions, based on solid data. The two most important discoveries to be made by a new trader is that trading consists of a decision making process whose actual consequence is unknown to the trader, and secondly, that any decisions made through this process should result from careful thought based on preparation and discipline.

However, one of the mistakes often committed by new traders occurs during the process of this discovery. Sometimes, inexperienced traders go through this process and discover that the decision was a good one and the trade is profitable. At this juncture, if the individual were to stick to his established rule of discipline, the trade would be exited at a specific point, cashing in on the profit produced by the correct decision. Unfortunately, when new traders realize that the trade they have just made is a winner and that it has also reached their target profit, they often break the rule they have established for themselves and wait to realize additional profit from the trade.

Sometimes this strategy works and sometimes it does not. The real damage that can be inflicted in this scenario occurs when the winning trade reverses itself into a loser. Sure, some trades succeed, others do not, but it seems the psychological damage most difficult to deal with results from the realization that you had a sure winner in your grasp and let it slip away. It is much easier to deal with the effects of a trade that was a loser from the outset; sometimes trades just don't work. However, knowing that you had a winner and letting the winning edge slip away is just too much to bear, especially if you end up losing money in addition to the unrealized profit that is gone forever once the trade is exited.

How does a new trader guard against this type of possible psychological devastation? Follow your rules, it's that simple. When you make a set of rules to govern your actions in the pit, use them for the purpose they are intended. What does it matter if you have a winning trade, reach your intended profit level, cash in your winnings and watch the trade become an even bigger winner? If you have followed your guidelines, you should already be back in the mix of trading, concentrating on your next trade. That rule which keeps you from allowing a winner to turn into a loser, can also stop you from allowing a loser trade to turn into an even larger loser. If you reach a predetermined level where you will take a loss, by following your rule, you will never allow yourself to lose more than you had intended.

Remember that winners never turn into losers when you stick to your guidelines.

SECRET #4
THE SCENARIOS OF TRADING

Depending on how you enter and exit the market, six basic scenarios continually appear. Regardless of the sequence of buying or selling, there are possible outcomes to making a trade: winning, losing, and scratching. Let's take a look at each of them.

BUY ONE – SELL ONE WINNER
The first, and probably the most logical to the majority of people, is this first scenario of trading. In this case, the trader will buy one contract, wait for the contract to gain in value from the purchase price and then sell the contract, resulting in a profit. The analogy of real estate is easily seen, if you equate the purchase of a house and then the subsequent sale of the house at some later time resulting in a profit for the initial buyer.

BUY ONE – SELL ONE LOSER
The second scenario is the buying of one contract then the sale of the same contract at a lower price. As statistically inevitable as the Buy One – Sell One Winner, this losing trade is, as we have stated a number of times in our text, a trading fact of life.

BUY ONE – SELL ONE SCRATCH
The occurrence of this scenario in the world of trading is quite common. Often a trader will purchase a contract at a specific price and subsequently sell the contract at the same price, because neither supply nor demand has moved the contract's price in a specific direction. A good trader, constantly monitoring the possibility of price movement, will many times buy a contract and sell it at the same price. This is known as a "scratch". He will then repeat the process over again, a number of times, hoping to anticipate price movement. He is trying to time his purchase accordingly, in order to sell the contract at a higher price, should the opportunity present itself.

SELL ONE – BUY ONE WINNER
At times, traders anticipate downward movement by selling a contract at a specific price, then purchasing it, later, at a lower price. This type of trade is also known as a selling short strategy, wherein the sale portion of the sequence of events transpires prior to the purchase.

SELL ONE – BUY ONE LOSER
In this case, the seller of the contract is unable to purchase it at a lower price; therefore, relegated to suffer a loss by purchasing the contract at a higher price, in order to exit the trade.

SELL ONE – BUY ONE SCRATCH
The trader initiates a sale and exits with a purchase, without a gain or loss from the trade.

Some would argue that, instead of the six scenarios presented here, there are just three, with the sequence of purchase and sale reversed. The main element of each, though, is the outcome, whether it is a gain, loss, or scratch. It is our hope that you, the new trader, intimately learn the nature of each of these scenarios and understand that each one is an integral part of the trading process. And remember, no matter which scenario the trader uses to enter and exit the market, he **MUST** check his trade with the opposite traders broker.

SECRET #5
OUT-TRADES

The purpose of this chapter is to introduce you to the secrets of trading. We want you to know the pit-falls of trading before they trip you up, and we want you to understand the nature of trading, to better prepare you for your first day. In this section of the secrets of trading, we will discuss an aspect of trading that is not an actual part of the pit process, but is nonetheless just as important as any element of the total process. We are referring to the out-trade.

An out-trade is the result of a miscommunication on the part of an individual during the course of trading. On most trading floors, outtrades are not discovered until a trade is entered into a computer and matched against the computer entry of the person with whom you have traded. An out-trade may result from any number of common mistakes by one party or both. The key to out-trades is to resolve them before they reach the stage where they are discovered as mismatched information in a computer entry.

When an individual makes a trade, he must record a number of pieces of information quickly and accurately. Once this is achieved, the trader moves on to his next trade. However, one secret to eliminating out-trades is to check with the person with whom you have traded as soon as possible, to restate the information you have recorded in opposition to theirs. In this way, if any discrepancies arise, it may be possible to resolve them before any changes have resulted from price movement in the market. If you check a trade immediately after its completion, you may be able to avert losses resulting from errors in communication. If market conditions are extremely volatile, the immediate discovery of an error may make a huge difference in its resulting cost. If a mistake is not discovered until the following trading day, the cost of a miscommunication, with prices significantly higher or lower, could possibly be large enough to end your career.

Therefore, one of the secrets to success in the trading pit is to check one's trades as soon as possible. This rule of conduct can be a significant help to avoid emotional destruction and unnecessary losses.

SECRET #6
KNOW THYSELF

It may seem odd to include this particular secret of trading in a text for new traders, but at some point in the career of the trader, this secret may become an invaluable tool for continued success in the pits.

As we have mentioned numerous times in our text, trading is a difficult yet rewarding task. It is both mentally and physically stressful and the toll can be great. It is for this reason we include this particular secret of trading—know thyself. By this, we mean that you and only you know when trading and the stresses it brings to bear on you become too much. You must know yourself well enough to recognize when your performance in the pit is suffering from the weight of the trading process. Only you know when it is time to get away from the rigors of work and rejuvenate your body and mind through a change in venue. In other words, one of the secrets to continued success in trading is knowing yourself and knowing when it is time for a day off.

Believe it or not, removing oneself from the pit is often easier said than done. There are two arguments that usually arise when vacation is mentioned. Together they form a vicious circle trapping the trader within. The first argument states: *I am making money consistently and I do not want to leave on vacation.* The second argument states: *I am not making any money and cannot afford to leave on vacation.* If these two arguments go hand in hand, then when do you take a vacation?

Well, if you are not performing up to the standards you have set for yourself and you suspect that your performance is suffering, then by all means, listen to your inner voice. If you learn to know yourself, you will know when it is time to take a break from the stresses of the profession. You must get away from trading, totally, too. No cheating by calling in to find out what is going on! We guarantee that quality time away from trading will, in the long run, positively increase your productivity.

Chapter IV
The Four Enemies of a Trader

In any endeavor, the real professional understands that his most ominous adversary is himself. Earlier in our text, we discussed the psychological aspects of trading and how they can destroy a trader when they are not understood. In this chapter, we will take a deeper look into what makes trading a simple process but a difficult proposition. We will examine those weaknesses directly related and most common in the trading profession. These destroyers of the psyche can be overwhelming to a trader, rendering him totally ineffective. So beware, for even the most well-balanced individuals may fall prey to the clutches of the following.

#1 OVERCONFIDENCE

There is no greater peril to a trader than the development of the foolhardy attitude that one's judgement is invincible. This is not to say that confidence is not a good thing. On the contrary, we have stated quite clearly that one must have a confident attitude in order to trade effectively. We have clearly shown what the result of hesitation can do to a trader. Those who lack confidence end up second guessing every move, resulting in more hesitation and further decay to the trading process. Confidence is a necessary asset to be a successful trader. However, what we are alluding to in this discussion is something far past confidence.

Many times, a trader will have a run of phenomenally profitable trading, where good decisions, based on a strong game plan and meticulous preparation, are rewarded with unimaginable results. Again, all traders know that they will make winning trades and losing trades, that's inevitable. But sometimes, traders hit streaks where the winning trades far out pace the losing ones, with results far out distancing expectations. At times like these, good traders, those with their feet on the ground, will step back and appreciate their good fortune, get back to the hard work of preparation and planning, and then re-enter the marketplace with a clear head and reasonable expectations in mind.

Unfortunately, some traders, who are the beneficiaries of this good fortune, begin to feel as though they will always continue with the same hot hand. Thus, **it is important to remember that each day is unique, unlike the previous one or the next to come.** Just because you have been trading well does not mean that the market will not reach up and drag you back to reality by the scruff of your neck, teaching you that no individual is bigger than the sum total of the market's participants. The message is usually swift and to the point: what the marketplace giveth, the marketplace may just as easily taketh. Overconfidence is a weakness that can turn a good trader into a bad one, even jeopardizing or ending your career.

#2 DISILLUSIONMENT

In opposition to the scenario of overconfidence resulting from good fortune, we would like to examine a syndrome common to new traders who are not quite as lucky.

In the initial stages of one's career, it is possible that a trader will do his homework, have a good plan of attack, do all of the right things, and still not succeed. You may go through a day making winning and losing trades, but, for some unknown quirk of fate, you seem to continually find yourself lagging behind on the profit side of the ledger. No matter how hard you work, there always seems to be one or two losing trades during the day from which you never quite recover. This type of misfortune may continue for days or weeks at a time. At no time do you ever lose control of your trading, nor do you fail to make good decisions. But, in the end, it is just a few, inevitable losing trades each day that stop your forward progress as a trader.

When this type of syndrome begins to affect a trader, behavior usually does not change in any way. However, psychologically, a person may begin to get down on himself for not succeeding. If the pattern is repeated, the self-doubt worsens. Finally, the notion may take hold that trading may not be a viable career. You must understand that all traders go through some form of this doubt about their abilities and trading at some point early in their careers. Do not let the seeds of disillusionment take hold in your mind. Believe that, given enough time and effort on your part, you will eventually reach your goals. Although doubt and disillusionment about trading will gnaw at you to give up, you nust adopt a positive attitude and continue to persevere to the best of your ability.

#3 PARALYZATION

For the new trader, one of the most difficult lessons to learn about trading is acquiring the ability to quickly react to a money losing decision. Many times, a novice trader will participate in a trade that immediately goes against him. Whether he is prepared for this inevitability or not, it is common for new traders to become paralyzed in this situation, unable to make the corresponding trade to exit the market, cutting his losses. There is an old adage in trading that states that your first loss is your smallest. What this means is that, the sooner you react to a losing trade, the smaller your financial penalty. If you become immobilized, unable to make the decision to accept your loss and quickly exit the trade, you are just making the situation worse. You must always be alert for this situation with a solution. **Think positively about your trading decisions but prepare for the negative – they will unavoidably occur.** If you get caught in a losing trade, you will have already planned out your escape route. Pinpoint the exact place you will exit the market, no matter how painful it is to realize the trading loss. Learn to extricate yourself, through your own trading efforts, or ask a floor broker to help you.

#4 DEVASTATION

When the downfall of confidence begins and descends to the level causing a total inability to make decisions, a trader may continue down this path of self-destruction until he reaches a level where he believes he cannot continue trading. He fears that every trade he makes will be a losing one. This self-fulfilling notion only worsens the situation, many times causing the trader to believe that his luck has abandoned him, forever. Unless you can keep reminding yourself that success comes through hard work and preparation, not luck, you may easily find yourself devastated by your inability to get back on a profitable track.

For the new trader, devastation can come quickly. New traders are under increased pressures not suffered by those traders who have already established their reputation as successful members of the pit. The novice must prove himself as a trader. He also suffers when he does make a losing trade that results in larger losses than usual, because he is relegated to trading small numbers of contracts. When unexpectedly large losses hit a new trader, inexperienced traders follow such occurrences with additional mistakes in an effort to recoup losses. New traders often fall prey to the error of adding to trades already losing money in the hope that the position will reverse the losses. Also, new traders will proceed too quickly to the next level of risk taking, jumping from a "one contract at a time" trader to a "five or ten at a time" trader, trying to make back their losses.

If this type of aforementioned behavior takes root, the black cloud of devastation will quickly descend, followed in short by total ineffectiveness caused by fear of further losses. When this stage is reached, you might as well turn in your badge and head for the exit, for you are no longer a participant in the business of trading, but a mere spectator of the opportunity unfolding around you.

It should be obvious from our discussion that the pendulum swings both ways. In times of good fortune and bad, there are enemies of the trader lurking in the shadows, waiting to do their damage. From the foolhardiness of overconfidence to the abyss of devastation and all that is in between, a trader must be aware of the psychological traps into which he may be ensnared. All do damage to the individual in their own way. Some of them, more permanent than others, but all negative in nature. It behooves the new trader to ready himself for the possible assault of this unproductive behavior.

Chapter V
The Ten Rules of Trading

Throughout our text, we have made mention of the fact that all good traders have a set of rules by which to conduct business. If you were to take a random sampling of these rules, you would invariably find the same ideas expressed in a number of different ways and listed in a different order of importance. However, no matter what the differences in wording or order, you would find that every trader has a definite method to his madness.

In this chapter, we take our years of experience and try to create a set of rules for you that will incorporate what we believe to be the most important concepts for conducting your trading. We hope that you take this list and shape it into a working set of rules for yourself, adding and subtracting your own ideas, until you have the best possible set of guidelines to help you in times of need.

Rule #1 DISCIPLINE IS THE KEY

No matter what the situation, the most important axiom of all regarding trading is that you must be disciplined. By discipline, we mean that, at all times, follow your list of rules to the letter. In theory, there are no exceptions to the rules that you adopt for yourself. When all others are losing their way because they are being affected by the emotion around them, you must not be moved to stray from the confines of your chosen directive; you make the rules, but you never break the rules.

As seasoned veterans of the trading pits, we have seen countless traders come and go. The one thing that remains constant concerning all of the individuals who did not succeed is the fact that they, for one reason or another, strayed from the common sense path of the rules they created for themselves. Some who failed were destined to do so, since they had no real game plan from the beginning, and never really were prepared for all of the possibilities confronting them. Others who failed were certainly intelligent enough to understand the process of trading and all of the nuances that arise from it, but they did not have the discipline to follow the rules they instituted for their own best interests. Perhaps these latter individuals were all the more tragic in their self-destruction, since all of the necessary tools were in place for success. Unfortunately, without the discipline required to stay in the game, the results were the same as those others who never really gave themselves the chance to succeed from the outset.

We cannot stress enough the need for adherence to basic, fundamental trading rules—they are the difference between success and failure.

Rule #2 ALWAYS GET THE EDGE

This second rule is so basic, that after a short while in the marketplace, you will not even refer to it, since it will be so ingrained in your trading mechanics. The edge, as we explained in an earlier chapter, is the process of buying a contract on the established bid in the pit and selling on the established offer. Since the bid and offer can change rapidly during the normal course of a trading secession, you must always be aware of who is biding to buy a contract and who is offering to sell contracts, so that you can take advantage of any change in the market as soon as it looms imminent. Thus, your whole focus as a trader is to get the edge. It is why you are paying to be a trading member of the exchange. You are physically in the pit, working at all times, to buy a contract on the bid and sell a contract on the offer. Gaining the edge is your bread and butter.

What is the big deal about getting the edge? It is a reasonable question to ask yourself, since it does not seem like such a big deal if you buy on the offer and sell on the bid. It is true that there will be times when you make a losing trade and may have to give up the edge in order to cut your losses. But for the most part, getting the edge means that you are always trading from a position of strength. If you buy on the established bid and the market changes, you should at least have the opportunity to sell your contract to someone else (probably a floor broker whose market does not usually change as instantaneously as an independent trader's does) who is also trying to buy on the bid price. By leaning or relying on other bids to buy at the same price that you are, you try to assure yourself a scratch trade—where no profit, or in this case no loss is incurred—if the market forces you to give up the edge to avoid a trading loss. If you have sold on the established offer and you feel that the market will change making the offer the new bid to buy, having already gained the edge, you can purchase contracts on the offer before it becomes the new bid, again avoiding a loss.

Other than constantly maintaining your discipline, the second most important precept for a trader to remember is that you are to use your presence in the pit to buy on the bid and sell on the offer. By following this rule, you will always allow yourself to trade from the desirable position of strength in the marketplace.

Rule #3 CONCENTRATE ON ONE PIT

This may seem like common sense, but far too many beginning traders try to spread themselves too thin by trying to trade in more than one venue at a time. It is imperative that you concentrate your attention on one market at a time in your initial trading ventures. It is too much to ask a new trader to flit back and forth between different pits, trying to keep track of more than one product. It is not only unwise, but we feel it is extremely foolhardy.

Beginning a career in trading takes a great deal of intestinal fortitude. You will be faced with a number of difficult obstacles to overcome. You will not be openly embraced into a pit when you start your adventure and it will take you some time to acclimate yourself to a trading pit. If you are constantly being distracted by the necessity to go into another pit, you will eventually find that it is impossible to keep track of what is going on in any of the pits in which you are involved.

Rule #4 NEVER LEAVE THE PIT

Once you have chosen a pit to trade in and reconciled yourself to the fact that you are going to trade in only one pit at a time, you need to set a regimen for yourself regarding the amount of time you will spend in the pit each day. Our recommendation is that once each trading session begins, you stay in the trading pit until the final bell sounds to end trading for that day. There is a very simple reason for the institution of this rule—if you are in the pit all day, you will always be on hand for any occurrence that might take place.

If you train yourself to stay in your spot in the pit all day long, you will always be aware of the bids and offers around you. You will have the advantage of the continuity that staying the entire trading session affords, because, by not leaving the pit, you will always be aware which brokers and traders are bidding to buy and offering to sell. Also, you will always be at the ready, if an order enters the pit that changes the trading dynamics.

When large orders to buy or sell contracts enter the marketplace, sometimes out-of-the-ordinary events occur. If you are taking a break or having a bite to eat or going to the bathroom, you may miss a golden opportunity that may not repeat itself. Remaining in the pit from opening bell to closing bell gives you the advantage of knowing what is going on at all times, while keeping the possibility open that you may participate in a trade that is a rare opportunity available only to the traders who are on hand at that very moment in time. If you stay all day, you will never be guessing about what has happened or wish you had been present to participate in a trade long since completed.

You must do whatever it takes to prepare yourself for a continuous day in the pit. Make sure you are completely armed with the tools of your trade before you enter the arena. Take care of your physical needs and learn the best way to ready yourself to stay in the same place for the entire session. If you can overcome the difficulties presented by this rule, you will benefit greatly by adherence to it in the long run.

Rule #5 ALWAYS TRADE IN YOUR COMFORT ZONE

This basic tenet of trading can be compared to the old adage of *"never bite off more than you can chew."* What the sages of the past were telling us with this simple, yet compelling statement is, never take on more than you can handle. This advice holds true, even when applied to trading. When you begin your career, start out with contract amounts that are comfortable for you and your financial situation. No one wants nor expects you to step into a trading pit and begin to trade one hundred contracts at a time, along with the risk that each trade of this magnitude entails.

A general fault of new traders is that they see other, established veterans trading contracts in large numbers and they want to join in at this level. What the uninitiated does not realize is that it takes experience to handle that type of trading. It is great if you happen to be correct in your anticipation of the market situation, but if you are wrong, trading large numbers of contracts to begin a trading career is one of the surest ways of ending your career quickly.

The idea of trading is to make a one-tick profit on a hundred trades rather than a hundred ticks profit on one trade. The job of the pit trader is not to speculate, but to take advantage of the bid/offer differential in the pit, with the aim of getting the edge, buying on the bid and selling on the offer, as we stated in rule #2.

Therefore, your technical function in the pit is to gain the edge and anticipate market movement only when you are forced to do so. If the market were not to move for long stretches of time, you would continue to buy on the bid and sell on the offer all day long, turning a profit, without speculating on which direction the market will head.

Your comfort zone should be buying and selling a small number of contracts to begin your trading. Your goal is to progress to larger numbers only when you are perfectly sure that you can deal with the increased pressure of the additional risk involved. If you stay in the zone of comfortable trading that this type of risk management affords you, you will never endanger your ability to return to the marketplace for the next day's trading session.

Rule #6 NEVER ADD TO A LOSING POSITION

To a new trader, this rule is a necessary addition to a list of essential guidelines on how to conduct business. All too often, a trader finds himself confronted by the decision of whether or not to buy or sell additional contracts, adding to an already existing long or short position. *How does one assess the situation correctly? Is there an established way of handling this situation if the position is either making a profit or showing a loss?*

Truthfully, each individual case has to be judged by its own merits. In most instances where you have a position showing a profit, you could add to the position, as long as you felt certain you could liquidate the position and realize the profit you have in it. However, the opposite situation is not as easy to assess, due to the psychological implications that accompany it. Unlike having a profitable one, a losing position often causes a trader to want to add to it, hoping to make back the losses more quickly by "doubling up." If the market turns in the right direction, the trader can make back his original loss by averaging a better price for the contracts he has bought or sold. But, many times, the trick of "doubling up" only ads further losses to an existing one.

If you find yourself buying or selling more contracts, all the while knowing that you are just making your losses worse, stop what you are doing. If you are waiting for an opportunity for prices to turn around to allow you to recover your losses, stop what you are doing and remind yourself about this rule. In essence, you are only lying to yourself, hoping that the market will not punish you for not taking your losses as soon as possible. Hope, in this business, will never get you anywhere. The first gradation of loss you suffer is always the cheapest—after that, the losses get worse and worse. Never add more to a position already producing losses.

Rule #7 NEVER LET A WINNER TURN INTO A LOSER

In the best of all possible worlds, every time you make a winning trade, it forever remains a winning trade. Unfortunately, in the real world, this is not always the case. Sometimes, you may do everything right when executing a trade and you may realize the fruits of your labor by cashing in for a profit. Their will be times, however, when a trade that is a winning trade one moment may become a losing trade the next, due to adverse market movement. This is not the type of trade that this rule addresses, for this situation confronts all traders from time to time. What this rule cautions is not to let a trade that you have executed and realized a profit become a losing trade through your greed to realize more profit than you should from it.

Since you will always be trading to get the edge—to buy on the bid and sell on the offer—most of your profits will be predetermined by the differential of the existing bid and offer. However, if the market should move in your favor after initiating a long or short position, you may be tempted to hold on to a position a little longer, to realize a bit more profit from it. That decision in itself is not a bad one, if you set a specific, reasonable goal for your profit taking. If you set an unreasonable a target that is never realized, you will have lost opportunity, especially if the once winning trade erases your existing profit, turning a winner into a loser. As we mentioned in an earlier chapter, this seems to be the hardest of all losses to accept. It is for that reason we establish this rule, with the hope of eliminating this devastating psychological damage.

One way to avoid breaking this rule is to set reasonable profit expectations for yourself. Pick a point at which to realize your profit and take it. If the trade turns out to have had more profit than you expected after you have already exited the trade, forget about it and move on without bemoaning the fact. If you stick by this rule, you will always be a winner.

Rule #8 BE A FLEXIBLE TRADER —BUY AND SELL, SELL AND BUY

Unlike the general public, a trader must be able to maneuver from either side of the market. The concept of short selling is most misunderstood by the investing population, and when applied to stocks, it almost seems unpatriotic to have a strategy that is based upon downward movement or unfavorable results for stockholders. The pit trader's primary function is to maintain a two-sided market, consisting of both a bid to buy and an offer to sell. It is easy to see how, in this context, a pit trader might first sell a contract and later buy it, offsetting his initial transaction and completing a round trip.

Do not make the mistake of becoming a trader who can only function in one direction. Adaptability is a hallmark of a successful trader. If you sense a market change is taking place and you have bought a contract on the bid, (getting the edge in the process), it may be necessary to sell that contract. In doing so, you have given up the edge in anticipation of a new market in which a new bid is established and the former bid has now become the new offer.

The reverse may be true in an upwardly moving market. You may have to sacrifice the edge, by purchasing a contract on the offer to sell, if you feel that the offer to sell may soon become the next bid to buy. Again, the versatile trader who expects to succeed must be able to adapt to the movement in the market. While always attempting to maintain the advantage of the edge of the bid/offer differential, a trader must be able to buy and sell, or sell and buy to complete a round turn transaction.

Rule #9 YOU MUST PARTICIPATE TO BE A WINNER

One of the greatest downfalls of the novice trader is the fear of participation because it might result in a trading loss. Since no one really knows for certain if buying or selling at any given moment is a winning or losing proposition, then how does one motivate one-self to participate in a trade? The fear suffered by a new trader can only be quelled by the act of participation in the trading process itself. Again, we revert back to the rule that urges the trader to get the edge, for there is safety in numbers, and having the advantage is always a positive.

No one has ever gotten wealthy or been successful at trading by standing in the pit watching the other traders buy and sell con-tracts. You too, must take the risk of losing money to make money. It is as simple an equation as no risk equals no loss and no possibil-ity of gain. There are traders who find themselves trading large volumes of contracts each day with no profits to show for their efforts. It is not as though they have made bad trading decisions, but there is a force at work that precludes them from making prof-itable trades.

The singular reason for you to enter a trading pit is to turn your ability to assume risk into profits. Your function is to trade and make money. Unfortunately, for certain traders *i.e.,* the tradeaholics, the game becomes more important than the end result. When mar-kets are not conducive to getting and maintaining the edge in the pit all day, some traders forge ahead and trade, regardless of whether or not they can acquire the advantage of the edge. Yes, as we said, participation is essential in being successful, but there are times when it is better to be more selective about participation. During market conditions when the best that one can hope for is breaking even, tradeaholics race ahead to participate, ignoring the underly-ing motivation of why a trader is trading in the first place. Always trade to make money; trading is not for fun and games, but a means to a livelihood.

Rule #10 WATCH, LISTEN, AND LEARN

Finally, each and every time you set foot in a trading pit, prepare yourself in every way possible to succeed. No successful trader ever enters the trading pit without a game plan. No successful trader ever begins his trading day without the best preparation he can amass. No successful trader ever buys or sells a single contract without knowing what to do if the unexpected may confront him. In essence, if you want to last in the trading business, a lot of hard work must precede your entrance into the pit each day.

With that in mind, you must also be ready to use your senses and intellect once you are in the trading arena. You must use your vision to scan the pit and notice when a broker turns to receive an order prior to his execution of it, for your visual readiness will far out-strip anyone else who waits to hear an order announced. You must listen and remember who is "bidding to buy" and who is "offering to sell" contracts so that you may turn to them in an instant to complete a transaction with them, if necessary.

In addition to the entire stimulus, you must learn the personal quirks of traders and brokers around you. If anything they say or do can help you to anticipate their actions to give you an edge, you must ingest this information and use it at the appropriate time. If you see others around you making miscues and errors, you must also remember and learn from their mistakes, so that you do not fall prey to the same misjudgments.

We hope that this discussion gives you a sound foundation on which to build your *pit persona*. We believe these ten rules are sound suggestions that will be most useful in promoting a successful trading career. Take them and the essence of the ideas they represent and restate, refine, and reconfigure them into a working set of guidelines for your own use.

SECTION VI
A Typical Trading Experience

Chapter I
A Day in the Life of a Seasoned Trader

Most people believe that all traders work for only a few short hours a day and make thousands of dollars with little or no effort. If the truth were known, a trader's day is shorter than most corporate hours, but that is only in reference to actual trading time in the pit. For all those who make their living in the pits, the entire effort put forth to make a day successful is long and arduous.

The following is a typical scenario for most traders. Since we are based in the Chicago markets and have experienced the daily grind of this particular existence, we will combine our daily routines to give you a realistic, honest insight into the average day of a commodity trader at a Chicago exchange.

THE PRODUCT

Let us assume that you are a trader in the **Standard and Poor** (S&P 500) Composite Index of 500 stocks. The daytime trading session begins at 8:30 a.m. and ends at 3:15 p.m., CST, coinciding with the opening and closing of the **New York Stock Exchange**. The S&P contract is a weighted index of 500 different stocks; mostly NYSE listed companies, together with some Amex and over-the-counter stocks. All trading takes place in 10 point increments (also known as ticks). Therefore, if the market moves from 1225.30 to 1225.40, a trader who has purchased a contract at 30 and sold it at 40 will have reaped a profit of $25.00.

YOUR HOME

The **Chicago Mercantile Exchange** is situated in the financial district of downtown Chicago commonly called "The Loop." The reference is to the elevated trains, which run in a circle around the outskirts of the center of the city. Although there is housing available within walking distance of the exchanges, for our discussion, let us assume that you are living in a neighborhood approximately 4 miles north of the heart of the city, known as Wrigleyville. Your neighborhood is approximately twenty minutes by subway, thirty minutes by bus, or ten to fifteen minutes by taxi or automobile to the heart of the financial district.

YOUR DAY'S BEGINNING

Typically, you hear the call of the alarm around 6:15 a.m. There is much to do to prepare yourself both physically and mentally for the ordeal awaiting you, hence the early rising time. After your usual regimen of hygiene, you dress in clothes that will allow you to function in comfort in the cramped spaces of the trading pits. Unlike **Corporate America**, the Chicago exchanges realize the physicality of trading and have amended their dress codes to allow for attire more conducive to the nature of the task at hand, unlike the **New York Stock Exchange** or the **London Exchange**, that still require a suit beneath a trading jacket.

Before the opening bell, you must also nourish yourself adequately, since the odds are you will not have much of a chance to do so during the seven hour span from opening to closing. Most of us have heard how important breakfast is as a meal: the wisdom of this information is extremely pertinent to the professional trader. You must be at your best when you step into the arena, and good nutrition is one essential part of the equation. Your job is to focus on the market, not on a growling stomach, or anything else; your concentration must lie only on the trading taking place around you.

YOUR TRIP

After seeing to your basic physical needs, it is 6:45 a.m. You start your daily preparation by switching on your personal news beeper to determine the present level of the Globex market, the electronic, off hours trading vehicle of the **Chicago Mercantile Exchange**. You must want to ascertain the range of the Index in relation to the previous day's settlement price, during the hours the exchange was closed. This initial action is followed by turning on the television to **CNN**, for updates on foreign markets. Finally, you search for an indication of opening U.S. Treasury Bond Prices, a market that in most scenarios affects your own marketplace. All of these tasks are performed ritually, since it is imperative that you are aware of where the market is currently trading and where the market has traded since you stepped away from the trading pit at the previous day's closing bell.

Satisfied that you have all of the information you need, it is time for you to hail a cab and head downtown. While others read paperbacks, magazines, or the sports section on their way to work, you do your best to familiarize yourself with any news contained in the **Wall Street Journal** that might affect the S&P 500 contract. With an attitude reminiscent of the ancient gladiators who also put so much on the line each time they entered the arena, you begin to feel an anticipatory rush with each mile you draw nearer to the exchange.

Reaching your destination at 7:15 a.m., your first stop is the Member's Information and Reception Desk. This facility is designated by the exchange as the place where each member may obtain computer generated sheets that show those trades, executed by the member on the previous day, that have cleared (agreed in all aspects with opposing brokers and traders) and those that have not cleared (those out of agreement —known as out-trades). Gathering all sheets identified with your acronym, your next stop is the office of your clearing firm. There, along with a daily statement—a record of all the trades that you executed the previous day, you will review the problems identified by the exchange's computer run and compare them to the information you recorded for each trade.

Faithfully, continuing your daily routine, you sit down to review your firm's record of each trade for the correct number of contracts, price of execution, and correct expiration month for each trade. Since you are using trading cards that have a tear-off carbon, you have collected a running total of each trade during the day, by saving the carbon copies. These tear-off sheets are then matched against your clearing firm's records. Your clearing firm keeps these daily records for you, for a predetermined charge.

Satisfied that your clearing firm statement has correctly recorded all of your trades for the previous day and your profit or loss is what you anticipated, you make one last check to be sure that each trading card had noted the time of day the trade was executed. The **Chicago Mercantile Exchange** requires that each trade is earmarked for time of execution by designating a letter of the alphabet or a symbol to correspond to 15 minute intervals noted by the trader for each trade. For example, any trade made between 8:30 and 8:45 is labeled with the letter G, 8:45 to 9:00, the letter H, and so on. Compliance with the exchange's demand for letter bracketing is important, since a heavy penalty may be assigned to those not conforming to this rule. Time bracketing also pinpoints exactly when a trade is executed, which may be helpful in resolving disputed trades.

Once you have determined that all of the trades in which you participated are entered into your statement, along with the correct prices and bracket information, you don your trading jacket and arm yourself with a supply of trading cards, pens, etc., to last the extent of the trading day. Now it is time to go onto the trading floor and confer with your clearing firm's out-trade clerk. An out-trade clerk is a person whose job is to resolve any discrepancies from the previous day that might arise when an error is made in the execution of a trade. If a trader has recorded the wrong price, the wrong quantity of contracts, or any other number of possible variable elements of a trade. The out-trade clerk tries to resolve the error and cement the finality of the trade prior to the opening of trading for the day.

Even though the statement from your clearing firm matches the carbon copies of your trades, there is still no assurance that each and every trade you executed is totally confirmed. You already know this for a fact since you noted that you had out-trades listed on the computer sheet you picked up from the exchange. The truth is that your clearing firm records the information you supply, taken from the trading cards you submit to them during the course of the day. This information, both correct and incorrect, is entered into the firm's computers and printed as your daily statement. It is then routed to a central area (clearing corporation) where all of the clearing firm member entries are matched against each other for comparison. If you are guilty of an error, it will not be immediately known by your firm until the information they have supplied to the central computers returns with an out-trade designation. When this happens, it indicates that one of the parties to a trade has entered information that does not correspond with the opposing trader. You, as a trading member of the exchange, are obligated to reconcile an out-trade before the beginning of trading for the next session. Aware that you have problems, you seek out the employee of your clearing firm whose main function is to resolve all disputed trades.

Some out-trades are simple to resolve: the out-trade clerk simply matches the questionable trade with the correct information from the opposing side, *i.e.,* he will change your record of the trade to reflect the correct opposing broker or trader acronym, correct opposing brokerage house, correct expiration month, etc. These types of errors deal only with the details of a trade that do not alter the profit or loss. If miscommunication results in an out-trade that brings about profit or loss to the trader represented by the out-trade clerk, the clerk must first confer with his trader.

If an out-trade involves changing consequential information, such as the number of contracts that are in question, changing the price of the contracts, or changing whether the trader is buying or selling the contracts, the out-trade clerk may not make any concessions with the opposing side of the trade. He is not authorized to make decisions affecting profit or loss brought about by the miscommunication.

On this specific day, you have two out-trades. You confer with your out-trade clerk and are relieved to discover that one out-trade involves only the misrecording of the correct brokerage house. The other out-trade has a difference in the price at which the contracts were executed. Unfortunately for you, the opposing trader correctly wrote down the price, that he substantiates through a comparison of the time bracket the trade was executed. By using corroborating print outs from the exchange's computer system, that record time and sale prices for each trading bracket, he wins his case by proving that the price you recorded was never quoted by the exchange during that 15 minute interval. Therefore, you are forced to adjust the price. This price change will show a loss in your next day's statement. You realize that mistakes will be made; you resolve to be more careful in the future.

BEFORE THE OPENING BELL

It is now 8:00 a.m., and you have a few minutes before the opening bell commences trading for the day. You enter the pit and head for your usual spot. Having been in the S&P pit for a number of years, you have carved out a niche for yourself that suits your trading style. You are a few rows down from the top step, a spot that enables you to trade one to five contracts per trade. You are within a reasonable distance of the top step brokers who execute all of the incoming orders. Your spot also allows a good view of the entire pit. This location not only allows you to see and hear trades not taking place in your immediate area, but it also provides you with the visibility necessary to participate in those trades.

In the minutes that remain before the opening bell, you take some time to interact with other traders. Your personal feeling is that an individual should be cordial during non-trading times; however, once the bell rings to begin trading, it is *every man for himself*. The rules of social behavior in the pit are stripped to a bare minimum, but they are nonetheless followed. The only ingredient different from normal social interaction is an unswerving "ME FIRST" attitude. A trader lives and dies by his last trade. Therefore, he is not inclined to be helpful to another trader.

With the dispensing of social amenities behind you, you take the final minute to follow another one of your daily rituals: you check the closing Globex price, current U.S. Bond and Eurodollar price, foreign currency levels, and pertinent stock market information, all supplied by the electronic boards that line the walls of the exchange floor. Satisfied that you have all of the information you feel is necessary to begin trading, you steady yourself for the eruption of sound and movement that will soon engulf you.

THE OPENING CALL

Approximately one minute to 30 seconds before the market is to open, brokers in the pit try to get a preliminary indication of where the market may open. This is done very carefully, without divulging any actual information. One broker may indicate that he will definitely pay 30 for some contracts. Another broker may agree that he too, will certainly pay 30 for some contracts and will definitely sell some contracts at no lower than 60. The prices announced at this time are just general areas. The broker who indicates that he will pay 30 may have orders to buy at 40, 50, 60, or higher. The broker who alludes to a sale price of 60 may very well be authorized to sell contracts at 50, 40, 30, or even 20, for that matter. The object of this exercise is to try and determine a general area of price where buy and sell orders may converge to facilitate an opening range that will be fair to the customers participating in the opening. All of this posturing continues until a general consensus is reached. This is called an opening call. Beware! This is not binding, and it may not indicate any actual fact. You, as a seasoned trader, are aware that opening indications are just what they appear to be—indications!

THE OPENING BELL

Within seconds of the opening bell, the following flashes through your mind: I am confident in my abilities; I will follow my rules for trading; I am prepared for any scenario that may occur in the market; I must participate to succeed.

At 8:30, the market opens, and to the uninitiated, it may seem as though all hell has broken loose, but to you, it is just another day at the office. As you watch and listen for the exact level at which orders determine the opening range, you try to assess which way the order flow will push the market. You turn your attention to the floor brokers on the top step of the pit. A majority of the brokers are gesturing with their palms turned inward, toward their body, denoting that they are buyers of contracts. As the split second cacophony of the opening wanes slightly, you discern the same brokers loudly screaming 30 bid, 30 bid, in an attempt to be heard all around the pit. The pitch increases and the market intensifies. Then the brokers, unable to buy contracts at the 30 level, raise the stakes by changing their bids by yelling, "40 bid, then 50 or half bid (in the particular jargon of the S&P pit) for 100." The race to buy contracts in the S&P pit is on.

You extend your right hand in the air and yell as loudly as you can, "Half bid for 5, half bid for 5!" You too, like the brokers above you, are attempting to buy five contracts at a price of 1150.50. A nearby floor broker, one of those who was not bidding, announces that he will sell 100 contracts at 60. Another broker immediately buys 50 contracts from him. Instantly, you turn and say "Buy 5." You have started the day by giving up the bid/offer differential, or the "Edge" by purchasing contracts where they are offered, not where they are bid by the majority of orders and traders in the pit. Your intuition is proven correct when another broker buys the remainder of contracts offered at 60. The same broker then turns to the rest of the pit and announces that he will pay 1150.60 for another 2-5 contracts. Fortunately for you, he continues to attempt to buy more contracts by bidding 60. When he is unsuccessful in filling the remainder of his order, he begins jumping up and down while yelling, "70 bid for 25!" You offer 5 contracts at 80. The broker, unable to complete broker, unable to complete his order at the 70 level, buys 25 contracts from local traders, 5 of which are from you. You have completed your first round trip (one buy of 5 contracts and one sell of 5 contracts) and it has proven to be a winner. Your profit for this opening venture is $250.00—from 60 to 70, you earned $25.00 per contract or $125.00; 70 to 80, another $125.00, for a total of $250.00.

As the day progresses, you attempt to stay in touch with the overall flow of the market, as you buy on the bid and sell on the offer, trying as best you can to anticipate the market's attempts to move higher or lower. You are aware, from your preparation before the opening, that the charts indicate the price of the Index will be supported at a level of 1149.10, and will have some difficulty rising any higher than 1152.90. Since you are aware that no news is pending that might affect a rapid rise or decline in the market, beyond these two support, and resistance points, you feel fairly confident that the S&P Index will probably trade within the range indicated by your expectations for the day.

Your expectations are fulfilled by your previous day's preparation when the price of the Index trades within the parameters you identified. You spend the entire session doing your best to anticipate market movement within this range. You are successful, for the most part, allowing the orders to help you determine what to do.

At 3:15 p.m., the bell sounds, indicating the end of trading. In retrospect, you have traded the market from open to close, without a break—something you are quite used to doing. You also feel confident that you checked each of your trades, in order to significantly lessen the possibility of having an out-trade the next morning. As some traders make their way out of the pit, others stay and wait for the post-close session. The post-close is a two-minute extension of the trading day. It allows brokers and traders to make any trades they were unable to complete before the official termination of the day's trading. A quick tally of your trades determines that you need not participate. However, you stay and observe the action, since you feel that it may give you some insight for tomorrow. Finally, you leave the pit with a feeling of satisfaction and accomplishment.

AFTER THE CLOSE

Although the market is closed, you are not through for the day. After a quick trip to the bathroom, you head to the office of your clearing firm. Each day, when trading has ended, you usually retire to your office carroll to perform a number of tasks. Using software designed to reflect upon your trading day, you rate yourself in a number of categories, each enabling you to gain insight into your pit behavior and trading performance.

In regard to your trading performance, you tally your winners and losers to discover that you have had a profitable day. Out of 67 round trip trades, 20% were losers, 55% were scratches and the remainders were winners. As a veteran trader, you allow your winners to take on additional profit, while cutting losses efficiently.

After a half an hour or so of analysis, your post close homework is completed. You grab your workout paraphernalia and head to your health club for a workout and whirlpool. You realize that you must allow yourself an outlet to relieve some of the stress brought on by trading. You understand that it is imperative for you to find a way to work out the rigors of trading and release your mind from the difficult grind under which a professional trader finds himself. Therefore, you make it part of your routine to jog, swim, or work out at your health club.

THE REST OF YOUR DAY

After giving yourself a vigorous, 45-minute workout and a relaxing whirlpool, you dress and make your way home. It is near 6:30 and tonight you have decided to stay in and get a good night's sleep, because you have a feeling that tomorrow could be a busy day in the marketplace.

Dinner will be a low fat meal, followed by watching television for relaxation. You quickly check the news channels for any developments that might affect the market, and then complete your final preparation for the coming day. You bring out your detailed charts of the price movements of the S&P 500 Index. Starting with the addition of today's highest price, lowest price, and closing price, you make a determination of support and resistance levels. Support levels are prices where buyers traditionally enter the market that supports it from falling; resistance levels are prices where sellers traditionally enter the market, preventing it from moving higher. Confident that your support and resistance levels are accurate, you conclude your preparation. Finally, you are off to bed at a reasonable hour, because you know only too well that 6 a.m. can come oh so quickly.

Tomorrow, your trading challenges begin anew.

Chapter II
Winding Down:
What is the Answer?

After completing the preceding chapter, it should be obvious to the reader that each individual day in the life of a trader is a mixture of hard work, physical and mental stress, and a search for relief from those rigors, provided by a non-trading outlet. During the typical day in the life of our fictitious trader, we mentioned that a visit to the health club was an integral part of it. In this chapter, we will focus on this aspect of a trader's life, to make it clear to all potential traders, that you must absolutely balance a life of trading with a safety valve, a release of the pressure and frustration that can result from a day in the pit.

In this chapter, we will examine the various ways to counteract the pressure of pit trading. Here are a few suggestions to help you, the pit trader, balance your life.

PHYSICAL EXERCISE

Exercise, on a regular basis, is the most common and effective method of release from the pressure resulting from a day in the trading pit. Since most traders complete their work-related responsibilities before the rest of the working world, they are able to make use of health club facilities, swimming pools, and golf courses before they are crowded.

Through our own experiences, most of the traders with whom we are familiar belong to health clubs, the YMCA, or just exercise on their own. Everybody, trader or not, needs to exercise regularly, but, for a commodities trader, this advice is critical. As we have stated, trading is a grueling existence, with stress and strain on both the body and mind. An individual needs to find a way to repair the body and soothe the mind. We will not make any authoritative statements as to what exercise regimen you should follow. However, we do encourage some sort of program. Whether it is as informal as a walk around the block or as regimented as a program with a personal trainer, we encourage you to exercise. The key to this discussion is participation on your part; ours is a role of advocacy.

RELAXATION

Along with exercise, the body must also engage in some form of relaxation in order to wind down from the pressures of the day. We do not encourage relaxation in lieu of exercise, but in addition to it. Expending time and energy preparing to trade, actually trading in the pit, and completing your after trading tasks, requires counterbalancing. Even the most dedicated trader must reserve time to forget about trading and all of the implications resulting from it. No matter how difficult it may be to do so, the dedicated trader must set aside time each day to relax and concentrate on something else. Watch a movie, read a good book, or watch television to allow your mind to relieve itself of the burdens of the day.

In addition to those activities we have mentioned as possibilities for relaxation, we would like you to entertain one further option, that we consider much more serious and fulfilling: meditation. The type of meditation to which we refer involves deep breathing, inner stillness, and attainment of an alpha state of the conscious mind. With ties to traditional eastern philosophy, our belief is that this type of meditation, making certain allowances for Western culture, can be very helpful in bringing about a desired state of relaxation. Since our intention is to enlighten you to the possibilities of meditation, at this point in our text, we feel that our discussion should not delve too deeply into the specifics of this activity. However, let it suffice to say that we have already incorporated this particular type of meditation in our training classes.

The most important thing to remember is that, in the normal course of each day, you make hundreds of decisions, assimilate thousands of bits of information, and constantly ingest all of the activity occurring around you. Give your brain a rest!

TRADER TEMPTATIONS

WINE, WOMEN, AND SUBSTANCE ABUSE

Section 2, Chapter 1, refuted the comparison of a professional athlete or a famous rock star to a commodity trader. However, in truth, there is one important similarity: famous athletes, rock stars and commodity traders all bear the burden of being only as good as their last performance. When you spend the majority of your time facing this fact, you may search for ways of relieving the burden of pressure. The constant battle to be successful, and/or remain successful, forces one to seek ways to dissipate the inner tension.

A clear mind and a sound body are imperative to peak performance. If you are suffering the effects of over-indulgence, it is virtually impossible to compete against the brightest minds in the world, access and process a plethora of information instantaneously, and successfully execute your trades at an optimal level. In a profession which spins by at a dizzying rate of speed, over-indulgence *i.e.* wine, women, and substance abuse, guarantees a short tenure as a professional trader.

THE FINAL ANALYSIS OF BALANCE

As you have probably concluded from the discussion in this chapter, a successful trader is one who has balance in his life —a balance between his life on and off the trading floor. The success or failure of one's trading performance must not dictate one's behavior away from trading. A great trading day should not be celebrated by over-indulging; conversely, a terrible trading day, should not be soothed through over-indulgence, either. Learn to strike an even stance in regard to both.

Thus, realize that there are aspects of trading that may lead to undesirable behavior. Be aware of them, so as not to become a victim. You must know yourself and keep a vigil. Look for signs that you are not yourself; it may be that you need to take time off. Also, be aware if you are starting to miss days because you are too tired or too hungover to go to work. These are all signs that the pressures of trading are not being processed through a positive outlet. Finally, trading is a profession that requires the individual to maintain a work ethic that provides continuity in and out of the workplace. Keep a regular schedule, one in which you make time to do other things unrelated to trading. Just stay healthy, both physically and mentally.

SECTION VII
Some Final Thoughts About the Future

Chapter I
The Rise of Trading to a New Position of Importance

We predict that the business in futures and options will quadruple in the next decade. Arising from the needs of the small speculator, the business hedger, the institutional manager or banker, and a host of other participants, there will be a need for a larger playing field for all interested parties. These players, and others, will utilize a multitude of products, both well established and brand new, to achieve their goals. What has brought about this need for expansion and increased interest? The reasons are many.

REASONS FOR TRADING'S ASCENDANCE

THE WORLD PEACE DIVIDEND

An interesting reason for the phenomenal rise of the importance that trading has experienced in recent years is the present state of world peace. With less monies earmarked for defense spending since the fall of Communism, both the volume and the influx of available capital has increased on most exchanges. Also, a wider range of investment possibilities has been realized through the emergence of opportunity in economies which had never before been open to the rest of the world. These nations, neophytes to the ways of capitalism, have seen interest in their previously closed economies skyrocket with the opportunity that comes with the get-in-on-the-ground-floor mentality by which they have bee besieged. Coupled with interest in the newly industrializing Pacific Rim region and other Third World nations, (interest afforded through the access of around-the-clock-trading), it is no wonder that the once rather esoteric business of trading has reached uncharted popularity.

CHANGES IN TECHNOLOGY

With the advent of technology and the instant communication it provides, the markets of the world are no longer isolated from each other. Market participants in one corner of the globe intently watch the movements of competing economies. This ability to constantly monitor the drama unfolding in distant parts of the world has opened up the international financial community, affording opportunity for many who have never before participated in it. And, this newly found audience has spawned a number of interesting trends that have contributed to the ascendance of trading as big business.

THE BABY BOOMER DEMOGRAPHIC

Another reason for trading's increased importance is due to a population demographic. The single, largest block of the population, those born between the end of World War II and the 1960's, some 40 to 50 million "Baby Boomers," have reached an age where retirement looms in the not-so-distant future. A tremendous number of these Boomers have, over the past fifteen to twenty years, repositioned their spending to include investments which will become an important source of income to supplement Social Security and individual pension plans. Their entrance, as a dominant force into the marketplace, has exponentially increased interest in markets and the business of trading.

THE U.S. STOCK MARKET

Another major element contributing to trading's ascendancy to a position of importance has come directly from the highly successful U.S. Stock market. With the meteoric rise of the Dow Jones Industrial Average, a new generation of traders have emerged. These traders have educated themselves, actively participated in a volatile marketplace, and learned to make money. The success of these traders has sparked additional interest, continually increasing the number of participants in the market. It is our belief that commodity futures and options trading will be the next beneficiary of this bounty of interest.

ENTREPRENEURALISM

Finally, combining all of this new interest in trading with the opportunity afforded an individual through technology, it is no wonder that the seeds of entrepreneuralism should sprout in the "fertile soil" of the exchange trading floor. In this new atmosphere, individuals seem to have rekindled that spark of daring that once permeated this country's psyche. The business of trading is now considered a business unto itself, rather than a means to an end. Just as medicine, law, or education are deemed desirable career paths, trading has taken a place of prominence among them. People are willing to forgo the security of a guaranteed salary for the openness and opportunity of trading for oneself.

An entire section of the population who have embraced trading as a vocation unlike any who have come before them. Since we are living longer and longer, the eldest segment of society has taken a proactive approach to their portfolios. Many are taking on the responsibility of trading for themselves, no longer relying on others to make decisions for them. These individuals, through electronic access, are actively participating in the process.

(HIGHER EDUCATION)

This exuberance for trading and its potential rewards has even spilled over into our institution of higher learning throughout the United States. It is now possible to take courses and earn advanced degrees designed to educate oneself in the more sophisticated aspects of futures and options trading, even to the point of preparation for a vocation in the industry. These colleges and universities will be responsible for a continued growth in activity and in the preparation of potential investors.

Research at the university level, in collaboration with the exchanges, will ultimately benefit the marketplace with new ideas and new products.

Chapter II
The Future Form of Trading

With all of the previous factors working in favor of its rise to importance, it is patently obvious that the business of trading is an industry with a very bright future. The only unanswered question remaining is the form in which it shall exist. What are the possibilities? The pros and cons of each?

For the last 150 years, commodity trading has taken place in an open out-cry arena. No matter the situation, open out-cry has been and continues to be the most consistent, efficient, and dependable for of trading. This method has withstood the test of time: through civil conflagration, world wars, and global upheaval, the time-honored method of pit trading has borne the burden of proof, consistently rising above all problems to deliver the best vehicle for the distribution of risk.

Throughout the history of this method, Chicago has been a mecca for the types of individuals who were the underpinnings of this success. From the **Chicago Board of Trade, Chicago Mercantile Exchange**, the **Chicago Board Options Exchange**, and the **Mid-America Commodity Exchange**, open out-cry has been a way of life.

Above all, in these venues, open out-cry has succeeded under the most difficult of circumstances. The aforementioned individuals have never shirked from their responsibilities. They have always afforded the public stability in the transference of risk by exhibiting liquidity, efficiency, and honorablility in the marketplace, beginning with the smallest trader and extending to the exchanges, themselves. The rules, procedures, and integrity of the markets are distinctly fair, while allowing the outside participants the peace of mind that the **Clearing Corporations** of the exchanges afford, by standing behind each and every trade, treader, and trading firm.

In times of market chaos and upheaval, pit trading has continually risen to the occasion. It remains to be seen, with the anonymity afforded by a faceless computer screen, if participants in a market will all but disappear if the going gets rough. No matter how you electronically recreate a pit trading environment to simulate the real thing, you will never reproduce the equanimity afforded the customer when a host of risk takers gather in one place, instantaneously making decisions which generate fair and equal price discovery.

AN OPEN INVITATION TO FUTURE TRADERS

As active participants in the markets we so avidly endorse, we want to share both our enthusiasm for them and our belief in them. If you have any doubts about th superiority of open out-cry trading over the alternatives, we invite you to visit Chicago, the birthplace of commodity futures and options trading. You will witness the most successful entrepreneurial trading environment in the world. Once you become a believer, we hope that you return as a participant. We hope you share our enthusiasm and let others know that you experienced a unique way of life—the world of **Chicago's Futures and Options Trading**. We promise you an experience that you will **always** remember!

Chapter III
To Sum it all Up

Now our journey is complete. Our intent was to present a realistic interpretation of the business of trading as experienced from a combined forty year career. We have shared with you personal insights and insider secrets. Hopefully, the information imparted will enable you to make an enlightened decision about a trading career.

It should be obvious, from our overall presentation, that we remain advocates of an open out-cry format of on-the-floor-trading. Having investigated and experienced trading electronically, we continue to prefer the efficiency of the physical, face-to-face trading of the exchange floor. However, we do agree that there is a place for electronic trading as both an adjunct to existing markets and as a primary venue for certain products. However, at this point in time, our belief is that anyone wishing to participate in a fair and orderly marketplace—one that gives equal opportunity to all participants— will find the price discovery afforded by open outcry trading the most efficient of any available.

In summary, we have asked you to be honest in your assessment of that which has drawn you to such an esoteric enterprise. In return, we have removed the veneer of glamor which trading so naturally exudes and exposed it for its reality: a business of hard work and great rewards. If you choose to use the knowledge you have acquired from our effort as a means to better insight when trading electronically or through traditional venues, then your destination will have been well worth it for us, too.

Just Moved In!

 **UOT FINANCIAL SERVICES**

30 SOUTH WACKER DRIVE, SUITE 1003
CHICAGO, IL 60606 ❖ TEL 312-382-1982 ❖ FAX 312-580-8159

A New Full Service Clearing Organization
Call Today